A New Owner's
Guide to
MINIATURE
PINSCHERS

JG-119

Opposite Page: An adult Miniature Pinscher owned by Connie Volk.

The Publisher wishes to acknowledge the following owners of the dogs in this book: Lee Abraham, Nancy Anderson, Armando Angelbello, Linda Anthony, Wendy Boyette, Kim Brallier, Carol Carlson, Helen Chrysler Griene, Miles and Betty Cottle, Bobbie Crissey, Marilyn D'Errico, Ila Dombrowsky, Nancy Duke, Marilyn Fahner, Jacqueline O'Neil, Diane Guerino, Shelley Guthrie, Jean M. Hardy, Elaine Hicks, Gretchen Hofheins, Paul and Michelle Jonas, Vickie Jones, Holiday Kennels, Sharon Kingsbury, Irene Klobber, Max Lee, Pat Lee, Mary Ann Lutz, Milehets Min Pins, Tina Monninger, Velda Pearson, Donna L. Peity, Kay Phillips, Jan Plagenz, Lorraine Pope, Rose J. Radel, Bob Ruphine, Jack and Judy Schatzberg, Mary Simpson, Linda Smith, Gale Studeny, Sandra L. Swanson, Connie Volk, Barbara Zagrodnick

Photographers: Janet Ashbey, John Ashbey, Callea Photo, Carol Carlson, Helen Chrysler Griene, Miles and Betty Cottle, Bobbie Crissey, Ila Dombrowsky, Marilyn E. Fahner, Isabelle Francais, Earl Graham, Gretchen Hofheins, Max Lee, Jacqueline O'Neil, Robert Pearcy, Pets by Paulette, Kay Phillips, Jan Plagenz, Rose J. Radel, Chuck and Sandy Tatham, Karen Taylor, Ed Vinson, Barbara Zagrodnick

The author acknowledges the contribuiton of Judy Iby of the following chapters: Sport of Purebred Dogs, Identification and Finding the Lost Dog, Traveling with Your Dog, Health Care, Behavior and Canine Communication.

T.F.H. Publications, Inc.
One TFH Plaza
Third and Union Avenues
Neptune City, NJ 07753

Copyright © 1997 by T.F.H. Publications, Inc.

ISBN 0-7938–X

Printed and bound in the United States of America

www.tfh.com

A New Owner's Guide to
MINIATURE PINSCHERS

Jacqueline O'Neil

Contents

1997 Edition

Min Pins are rugged outdoorsmen as well as superior snugglers.

The Miniature Pinscher is small in size, but big in character.

Proper socialization of your Min Pin puppies will make them well-adjusted adults.

Male and female Min Pins are equally as enjoyable as family pets or show dogs.

The Min Pin's regal disposition is why he is called the "King of Toys."

HISTORY of the Miniature Pinscher

ave drawings from 50,000 years ago show men and dogs hunting together, and archaeologists agree that dogs were the first animals domesticated by man. The earliest dogs protected the campsite and helped primitive man find and kill other animals for food. Later, as man became civilized enough to domesticate a variety of animals, dogs began guarding flocks and herds and serving as beasts of burden.

Small dogs, such as Miniature Pinschers, have existed as far back as the Stone Age, according to archaeological studies.

ANTIQUITY

By studying Egyptian tombs from the period around 3700 BC, archaeologists found that some dogs were worshipped as gods and buried as mummies. Drawings of several types of dogs were discovered on royal tombs. From these images, it appears that the early people of the Nile Valley had dogs of four major body types. In addition to the greyhound-style dogs usually attributed to them, they also had short-legged terrier-type dogs, large dogs with massive heads, and small dogs with erect ears and tails that curled over their backs.

Archaeological studies in Europe have unearthed canine skeletons, which proves that tiny dogs existed as far back as the Stone Age. During the 1800s, when pure breeds were finally established, these ancient tiny dogs played a part in the ancestry of several toy breeds.

The Toy Group, of which the Miniature Pinscher is a member, is made up of small companion breeds from all over the world.

CLASSIFYING CANINES

Classifying dogs as individual breeds is quite modern. Before the 19th century, dogs were classified according to the work they did. Later, when the concept of breeds first became established, it described the dog's purpose, not his appearance. The word "terrier," for example, was used to describe dogs that hunted by digging their quarry out of the ground. In those days, a terrier was considered purebred if both of his parents hunted in the same way. Whether or not the sire (father) and dam (mother) resembled each other physically didn't matter at all.

Eventually, people bred dogs that excelled at a particular job to other dogs that performed well at the same task, and selective breeding came into being. After many generations, dogs from a certain area of a country that were bred for the same function began to resemble each other and share similar behaviors. That's how the foundation stock for today's multitude of breeds was established.

Today, dogs are still divided by function when it comes to the American Kennel Club's seven groups: Sporting, Hound, Working, Terrier, Toy, Non-Sporting and Herding. The Toy Group, of which the Miniature Pinscher is a member, is made up of small companion breeds from all over the world.

GERMAN BEGINNINGS

The dog that modern history assures us is the early Miniature Pinscher was originally called the Reh Pinscher. He was so named because the Germans thought he resembled the nimble, small, red roe deer that populated their forests. Dog shows were officially considered a sport in Germany in 1863 and the first mention of Reh Pinschers in the show ring was published in a 1876 show report.

Part of a family simply called the German pinschers, the Reh Pinscher was the smaller version of a more common, medium-sized dog that was known since the 16th century as the Deutscher Glatthaar Pinscher or the German Smooth-hair Pinscher. The larger variety was popular for use on farms, as he was good at controlling rats and mice in the barns. The smaller pinscher was also a good ratter and mouser but usually performed his job inside the home. In fact, it is generally believed that the name pinscher was taken from either pincer or pincher in the English language, and referred to the dogs' tendency to kill vermin quickly by grabbing and holding fast.

In addition to size, there was another distinction between varieties in the German pinscher family. Dogs with longer coats were designated wire-haired, and Schnauzers of various sizes, as well as Affenpinschers, were considered Wire-haired Pinschers. Those with short hair, like our Miniature Pinschers, were called

smooth-coated. During the mid-1800s, when German fanciers first tried to separate the varieties within the

Early Miniature Pinschers were called Reh Pinschers by the Germans because they resembled the red roe deer.

Contrary to popular belief, Min Pins are more than just lap dogs. They are rugged little dogs that enjoy spending time outdoors.

pinscher family, they discouraged breedings between the two coat types.

The serious pinscher breeders established the Pinscher-Schnauzer Klub in 1895. They recognized six varieties of pinschers for registration and demanded that the varieties not be cross-bred. Recognized breeds were the Giant Schnauzer, Standard Schnauzer, Miniature Schnauzer, Affenpinscher, Old Standard German Pinscher and, of course, the Miniature Pinscher.

POPULARITY PLAYS HAVOC

The smallest pinscher gradually became a favorite in the show ring, and soon his booming popularity played havoc with the breed's soundness and usefulness. There were no specialist or breeder-judges for the little Rchs, so they were often evaluated by sporting dog judges. Accustomed to evaluating large hunting breeds, these judges apparently believed that little dogs were only useful as ladies' lap dogs. Soon Miniature Pinschers competed in the show ring, decked out in ribbons and jeweled collars, and were judged in their owners' arms or sitting on satin pillows. Movement and soundness were not even evaluated since the dogs' feet never touched the ground, and the only features the judges considered were smallness and a pretty head. Tininess soon became the fashion and breeders sacrificed every attribute of the breed in their haste to produce the smallest dogs. It wasn't long until this practice led to degeneration in the breed. Soon, Miniature Pinschers were incredibly tiny, with pitifully weak structure and scrawny, feeble legs.

Josef Berta, a respected judge and one of the founders of the Pinscher-Schnauzer Klub, decided to put an end to this nonsense. Whenever he judged, he demanded that the toy dogs be placed on the ground and moved in the same gaiting pattern as the big dogs. If a specimen wasn't sound, he didn't win.

This muscular Min Pin is a perfect example of the strength and soundness that Josef Berta sought in order to save the breed.

Berta's method upset some of the breeders so much that they stopped showing rather than put their delicate dogs on the floor. However, the associations that held dog shows kept hiring Berta. In fact, they assigned him the toy breeds so often that today he is credited with saving the Miniature

When Min Pins first appeared in show rings, they were judged in their owners' arms or on satin pillows. Today they are evaluated on soundness and movement as well as beauty. This is Am/Can Ch. Goldmedal Midnight Star, owned by Barbara Zagrodnick.

Pinscher by bringing soundness, balance and mobility back to the breed.

For several years prior to World War I, the Miniature Pinscher, thanks to Berta and his followers, became healthy, balanced, sound and beautiful, still retaining his popular appeal. Historians call the period around 1910 the breed's "Golden Years." During that era, as many as 60 splendid and fit Miniature Pinschers could often be found competing at one show.

EFFECTS OF THE WAR YEARS

World War I did tremendous damage to the breed. Because food was difficult to obtain, the German people found an alert and brave small dog easier to maintain than a larger watch dog. Demand for the breed was high, and high demand always entices the type of breeders who care only for money and make no effort to produce quality dogs. These profiteers gladly met the demand by breeding a multitude of inferior dogs. As these poor specimens were bred to other deficient dogs, the breed soon

Despite the loss of soundness that resulted from excessive breeding in Germany during WWI, responsible breeders saved the Miniature Pinscher by restoring their breeding programs. deteriorated. By the end of the war, many Miniature Pinschers were weak and timid, and the German Kennel Club wisely refused to register the breed until it regained its soundness and spirit. Unregistered dogs don't bring much money, so the profiteers lost interest in the breed, leaving its loyal supporters the task of repairing the damage.

With the help of Judge Berta, the responsible breeders prevailed again. "Power and Warmth" became the slogan for their breeding programs as they attempted to correct their beloved breed's ills and recreate a healthy, sound and confident small dog. By 1924, German experts were once more praising the breed.

The Miniature Pinscher's seesaw struck the ground again when World War II also caused excessive popularity. The profiteers returned and thousands of sad specimens were produced, resulting in another decline in quality. Besides small, weak specimens, there was a proliferation of larger, coarse dogs. However, recovery was rapid following the war because many devoted fanciers had continued breeding excellent stock and the Pinscher-Schnauzer Klub tightened its regulations. Before litters were permitted registration, they were evaluated by an expert and puppies had to be of good quality to rate their papers. During the year 1945, only 76 Miniature Pinschers were accepted for registration. A sign of the breed's quick recovery is that in 1947, 705 Min Pins were added to the record.

Though they appear to be a smaller version of a Doberman Pinscher, the Min Pin is actually an older breed than the Doberman, recognized some twenty years earlier.

NOT A MINIATURIZED DOBERMAN

The Miniature Pinscher is not a bred down or miniaturized version of the Doberman Pinscher. Actually, the Miniature Pinscher is an older breed than the Doberman Pinscher and was first recognized as an official breed in Germany in 1880. The Doberman Pinscher, which originated in Germany years later, was not officially recognized in its native land until 1900.

The persistent but false belief that the Miniature Pinscher evolved from the Doberman is probably the result of the standard written by the Miniature Pinscher Club of America in 1935. Under General Appearance, that standard said in part, "A miniature of the Doberman Pinscher, having on a modified scale most of its physical qualifications and specifications." The Doberman was more widely known in America than the Miniature Pinscher, so the authors of the standard probably thought that the toy breed would be more easily recognizable if they compared it to the more popular Doberman. However, later readers assumed that the meaning was historical, rather than simply descriptive.

In 1950, when the club revised the standard, the members
attempted to correct this confusion by removing all references to
the Doberman Pinscher. But the damage had already been done.
Even today, many people still wrongly believe that the Miniature
Pinscher is a scaled-down Doberman.

ADVANCEMENT IN AMERICA

Old family photographs that include Miniature Pinschers
prove that the breed arrived in America at least as early as 1900.
Like many breeds of foreign origin, the first dogs accompanied
their families when they immigrated to America.

The American Kennel Club accepted the Miniature Pinscher
for registration on March 31, 1925. A female named Asta von
Sandreuth, described as black, red and brown, was the first dog
of the breed to be AKC registered. She was whelped in Germany
on June 5, 1924, and was imported to the United States by her
American owner, Mrs. B. Seyschab. By 1929, the Miniature
Pinscher Club of America was recognized by the American
Kennel Club and Min Pins were entitled to compete for
championships.

The American Kennel Club originally designated Miniature
Pinschers as terriers, so they began their competitive career in
the Terrier Group. Nevertheless, the Miniature Pinscher Club of
America was not happy with that classification and petitioned
the American Kennel Club to reclassify the breed. A year later, in
1930, Min Pins were placed in the Toy Group and called the
Pinscher (Miniature). In 1972, the official name of the breed was
changed to Miniature Pinscher.

THE DEVELOPMENT OF THE AMERICAN STANDARD

At first, the Miniature Pinscher Club of America simply
translated and used the German standard for the breed. In 1935,
the first American standard was drafted. Size (weight and height)
eventually caused dissension in the breed club, and the standard was
changed to correct fads such as Min Pins that were too coarse or too
tiny. The entire standard was revised for the first time in 1950. The
current standard, approved in July of 1980 and reformatted in 1990,
includes a disqualification that should prevent future fads in size
changes. Ideal height is determined to be 11 to 11 $^1/_2$ inches at
the withers, and Miniature Pinschers must be between 10 and
12 $^1/_2$ inches tall to be permitted in the show ring.

The Popularity Problem Reappears

During the year 1950, 1,434 new Miniature Pinschers were registered with the American Kennel Club. In 1955, 2,353 more Min Pins were registered. Viva Leone Ricketts, a respected authoress, expressed concern about over-popularity and the indiscriminate breeding and inferior specimens that often result. This time, the breed withstood its season in the spotlight. Numbers leveled off quickly and the breed's quality was preserved.

Today we have a similar situation. With so many Americans living in apartments and condominiums, a stylish small dog with the alert attitude and brave demeanor of a large dog is very much in demand. In 1989, the American Kennel Club registered 5,568 Miniature Pinschers and the breed ranked 40th in popularity. Then, in only one year, the number of Min Pins newly registered with AKC rose an astonishing 46.8 percent. In 1990, 8,176 Miniature Pinschers were added to the registry and the breed

Because of its small size and vibrant personality, the Min Pin is becoming increasingly popular with each passing year.

15

jumped to 37th in popularity. By 1991, the Min Pin was the 33rd most popular breed with 10,772 new dogs added to the roster. The breed sprang to the 30th spot in 1992, prompting AKC Vice President John Mandeville to write in the *AKC Gazette*, "The most interesting Toy breed story is that of the Miniature Pinscher, which finished 1992 as the 30th most popular of all breeds, up from 33rd place in 1991. For the year, 13,353 Min Pins were registered—a 2,581 increase from the 10,772 recorded last year. This was a 24 percent rise for the year and a clear indicator Min Pins are on the upside of the fad breed roller coaster."

The modern Miniature Pinscher looks great and behaves like his nickname, "King of Toys."

Min Pin popularity made another jump in 1993 when 14,987 dogs were registered, ranking the breed 29th overall in popularity. But the increase in 1994 was even more spectacular. The breed was 23rd in popularity by the end of the year with 16,538 new dogs registered. Thus, in the five-year period from 1989 to 1994, Miniature Pinscher registrations increased a remarkable 197 percent.

FAVORABLE FUTURE

While some profiteering types have jumped on the Min Pin bandwagon, the majority of modern Min Pins look great and behave like their nickname, the King of Toys. The Miniature Pinscher Club of America is made up of dependable breeders representing the length and breadth of the country. In addition, many local breed clubs are dedicated to preserving, protecting and improving the breed.

With so many responsible breeders, you should have no trouble finding a fine Miniature Pinscher puppy.

You should have no problem finding a suitable Min Pin puppy for your very own if you do your homework.

CHARACTERISTICS of the Miniature Pinscher

Stylish and saucy, the Miniature Pinscher's proud carriage and regal gait have earned him the nickname King of the Toys. Often referred to as a big dog in a little package, this animated sprite has a bold aspect and is really quite brave. While every member of this breed has his own unique personality, certain characteristics should be apparent in every specimen.

VIGOR AND VALOR

The breed standard mentions the Miniature Pinscher's fearless animation, complete self-possession and spirited presence. These characteristics are as much a part of proper type as the dog's physical appearance. A correct Miniature Pinscher exudes self-confidence, not only in his own home or cradled in the safety of his owner's arms but also walking on lead down a busy street, passing other dogs in the park and at obedience school.

The Miniature Pinscher does not seem to realize that he is small and will approach even gigantic dogs in play, sometimes with aggression. Owners have to be cautious for their little dogs since Min Pins believe that they are a match for anything on four legs, and not all large dogs find this trait amusing.

Originally classified by the American Kennel Club as a terrier, the Miniature Pinscher still retains terrier-type tenacity. Urban dogs seldom have the opportunity to stalk anything

Four proud Min Pins posing for posterity and showing off the complete self-possession they're known for.

larger than a low-flying moth, but their rustic relatives still enjoy the chase and reportedly catch rabbits bigger than themselves as well as all manner of small rodents. While reveling in the hunt, they also have the persistence to wait out their prey and many of them exhibit the terrier tendency to determinedly dig their quarry out of the ground.

Though no longer classified as terriers, Min Pins will still stalk and chase rabbits or small rodents if given the opportunity.

Alert watch dogs with an inordinately keen sense of hearing, Miniature Pinschers recognize the sound of their owner's vehicles and footsteps, but are quick to bark a warning when strange cars pull up to the house or unfamiliar footsteps draw near. It is not unusual, or wrong, for a Miniature Pinscher to be somewhat reserved toward visiting strangers and

These lively pups are enjoying a play session, their favorite part of the day.

possessive about his human family. An ideal Min Pin, however, will accept his owner's friends within a reasonable time and soon demand some attention from them. When away from his home territory, the dog should be outgoing toward friendly strangers and inspect new places with fearless curiosity.

SMART AND SHOWY

Training a Miniature Pinscher is fun because the breed learns fast and has excellent retention. Some Min Pins are so clever that soon after they perfect a lesson, they become creative in finding new ways to perform it. To succeed in training a Miniature Pinscher, it is important to be patient, firm and matter-of-fact so your dog will be convinced that you are smarter and more composed than he is. Min Pins

Easily trained, the highly intelligent Min Pin learns fast, has excellent retention, and works hard to please his owner.

are terrific hams and relish praise, so keep the kudos coming and your dog will continue performing with obvious pleasure.

ENERGETIC AND ADAPTABLE

Highly adaptable, a Miniature Pinscher can be happy in a studio apartment or a country estate. Small enough to create an exercise path of his own in even the tiniest apartment, a Min Pin may suddenly take off on a madcap race and do several laps around the living room sofa. Min Pins also enjoy playing with children, provided the youngsters have been taught how to safely and gently handle a pet. Children should enjoy a Min Pin only with adult supervision until they are old enough to understand that dogs have intelligence and feelings, and are not four-legged wind-up dolls to be pulled and poked. Tiny dogs and toddlers are never a good combination.

Min Pins love to find a place to curl up. For this tiny pup, his owner's hands are just the right size.

The Miniature Pinscher loves warmth and is a superior snuggler. He will contentedly curl up on a pillow by the fireplace, in a loving lap or deep beneath the covers of your bed. However, Min Pins can handle a walk on lead during the winter, and a warm sweater that protects the chest and belly as well as the back is a good investment in colder climates. Owners who exercise their Min Pins by turning them loose in fenced yards should be careful not to leave their dogs outside long enough to catch a chill.

PERSONALITY TRAITS OF SUCCESSFUL MINIATURE PINSCHER OWNERS

The Miniature Pinscher certainly is an outstanding dog, but no breed is exactly right for everyone. While Min Pin owners are as original as their dogs, those who have enjoyed the breed for many years have a few traits in common. The Miniature Pinscher may be the best breed for you if you fit most of the following personality traits. But, if few of these qualities match your character, think long and hard before purchasing a Min Pin. There are over 200 other breeds of dog in the United States to choose from.

Confirmed Miniature Pinscher owners often have:

1. *Enough space in their schedules and their hearts to accommodate an accomplished lap-warmer*: Your Min Pin will be happy to watch television with you or help you read a book. He just wants some time near you every day.

2. *A strong sense of humor*: Just when you think your Min Pin has learned a particular trick or obedience exercise, he may come up with a clever way around it. Your Min Pin will eventually condescend to do it your way, but, in the meantime, you will enjoy training your imp a whole lot more if you secretly admire his creative talent and find him amusing rather than frustrating. A sense of humor will also serve you well if your dog decides to showcase his individuality in the obedience ring.

In order to have a happy, loving, lasting relationship with your Min Pin, you must be responsible, patient, and have a sense of humor.

3. *A bit of the child in them, no matter what their age*: The Miniature Pinscher retains his puppyish love of toys and games into old age and it isn't unusual to see a vivacious, gray-muzzled pup play-killing his favorite squeaky toy and proudly strutting around the room with it. Owners who share in the fun get the most enjoyment from owning a Min Pin.

4. *The ability to combine patience with persistence*: Min Pins make happy and willing workers, but because this breed is both inquisitive and clever, it can test the patience of the trainer. Seldom satisfied to do obedience work in the prescribed fashion, the Min Pin sometimes seems to try new things just to see his owner's reaction. Owners who stay calm and use patient persistence and lots of praise eventually end up with marvelously trained dogs.

5. *A sense of responsibility about keeping their pets comfortably housed indoors and safely confined when outdoors*: The Miniature Pinscher is a house dog. Unable to tolerate cold temperatures or drafty basements, he needs cozy quarters near his human family and can get enough exercise in an apartment. When allowed outdoors he should be in a

Inheriting much of their personalities from their confident and assertive mom, these puppies will grow to be equally as self-assured.

securely fenced yard with sufficient shade, shelter and fresh water, and when taken for a walk he should always be on lead.

6. *A special love for precocious pups, even though they may present more of a training challenge than dogs of lesser intelligence*: The Min Pin seems to be always thinking, and training one will keep you thinking too.

7. *A preference for exuberant dogs over placid types*: The Miniature Pinscher is curious, alert and joyful, with a high activity level and a well-developed sense of fun. But while the breed prefers an active lifestyle, it easily adapts to a more sedate household if acquired young. In fact, Min Pins are beloved pets for thousands of senior citizens.

8. *An eye that finds beauty in sleek, short-coated animals*: The short, shiny coat of the Miniature Pinscher needs little

grooming to stay glossy and clean. If you love the look and feel of fluffy dogs, and look forward to brushing and fussing, this isn't the breed for you. However, if you would rather spend your time petting and playing, you are reading about the right breed.

9. *A desire for a charming canine companion*: The Miniature Pinscher is first and foremost a companion. He is also an alert watch dog, and some members of the breed excel at competitive activities such as showing, obedience, agility and rewarding avocations such as therapy work. But besides knowing what the Min Pin is, it's also important to understand what this breed is not.

The Miniature Pinscher is neither a guard dog nor an attack dog. While he is sometimes an excellent ratter, this is not a hunting or sporting breed. A well-conditioned Min Pin will be delighted to accompany his owner on long walks in pleasant weather but will prefer his cozy bed on rainy evenings and frosty winter mornings. While this little dog is confident and brave, he is also vulnerable and sometimes has to be protected from his own brazen attitude toward larger animals.

Like most Min Pins, these puppies enjoy their warm, cozy bed. Min Pins have a perfect blend of exuberance and affection.

10. *Joy of life*: Living with a Miniature Pinscher is never boring. Extremely fun-loving, this dog greets each day with renewed cheer, and some owners swear that their dogs spend the night dreaming up new ways to tease. A happy, healthy Min Pin moves with quick, deft agility and never goes anywhere at a walk that can be reached at a run. He enjoys his toys, and whether his owner chooses to join in the games or simply watch, the spectacle is entertaining. With the spirit of a large working dog and a bark that is bigger than he is, the Miniature Pinscher is a fine small dog for anyone who wants a little one with the heart of a hero.

STANDARD for the Miniature Pinscher

Every breed has its own unique standard of excellence. Written by a parent club that represents and protects its own breed, and approved by the American Kennel Club or another legislating organization, the standard describes what the breed's recognized experts perceive as the ideal dog. To understand this concept, think of the Miniature Pinscher standard as a descriptive blueprint or word-picture of what constitutes an absolutely perfect Min Pin. Part of the breeder's challenge is the realization that such a flawless paragon never existed. Even in the best examples of the breed there is room for some improvement.

The breeder's art is the ongoing quest to create a dog that fulfills every aspect of the standard. The standard is just words, and words are open to interpretation, but good breeders study those words carefully to arrive at a mental picture of the ideal dog. Then, they try to produce dogs that come as close to their interpretations of the standard as possible.

Judges select dog show winners by comparing each dog in a competitive class to their own visualization of the perfect specimen as described in the standard. Since top winning dogs are often used for breeding, judges and breeders each play a role in interpreting perfection, and their decisions impact the breed.

When learning about a breed, it is essential to study its standard. Since standards often have terminology that is difficult for new fanciers to understand, the Miniature Pinscher standard is defined and explained in this chapter. However, you should first understand a few fundamental words that are always used when dogs are evaluated.

TYPE

Type enables people to immediately recognize what breed of dog they are looking at. It is all those features that combine to make a breed of dog look like that breed of dog and set it apart from every other breed. A *typey* dog is one that comes close to matching the characteristics called for in the breed standard, and the most typey dog in the conformation ring is the one which best satisfies the standard. Judges consider type exceedingly important since it differentiates between the breeds. Yet even among the most typey individuals, some variation and slight dissimilarities in height, substance, refinement or expression are to be expected.

Described as naturally well-groomed, compact, and animated, the Miniature Pinscher must also be fearless and alert.

Every knowledgeable breeder works with his own mental picture of perfection and tries to breed dogs that display his or her personal interpretation of shape, size and expression. As long as the dogs conform to the standard they will have type, but on close inspection they may look a little different from another breeder's ideal dog, which is also typey.

Breeders who ignore or who do not fully understand their breed standard run the risk of losing type. One sure way to destroy type is by exaggerating one section of the standard, such as the shape of the head, and disregarding the rest.

BALANCE

A dog is *balanced* if all of his body parts seem to fit each other and no part overwhelms the rest. A dog with a long, thin body and a wide head is not balanced, and a dog with a stocky body and a tiny head is also out of proportion. The word proportion is often used interchangeably with the word *balance*.

CONDITION

While you can't control whether or not your Miniature Pinscher will be typey or balanced at maturity, the dog's *condition* is completely controllable. *In condition* is the optimal physical state. It designates a dog that carries the right amount of weight for his size, has good muscle tone and clear eyes and has a clean, healthy coat that seems to glow from the inside out.

SOUNDNESS

A dog is *sound* if his body functions well. *Soundness* is comprised of a structurally correct skeleton, a reliable temperament, appropriate musculature and no impairments (physical or mental, temporary or permanent) that would impede the dog from using these attributes. Dogs are considered unsound if they are deaf, blind, unduly aggressive, exceptionally shy, highly nervous, lame or missing one or both testicles. A limping dog is not permitted to compete at a show because favoring a leg is considered unsound. If a dog limps because he skidded into a wall during play and bruised his shoulder, he is temporarily unsound. When the soreness goes away and the dog moves normally, he is sound again.

Not all faults in a dog are classified as unsoundness. If the breed standard calls for dark-colored eyes, a dog with light eyes is not unsound provided he can see out of those eyes. However, if light eyes are uncharacteristic of the breed, the dog would be described as lacking type. For an extreme example, a Miniature Pinscher might have a low tail set, a pink nose and an ear that droops, but as long as those parts are all useful, the dog is still sound. But because those features are in opposition to the Min Pin standard, the dog would be utterly lacking in type. The stray mongrel that breaks your garbage bag may be sound, but mixed-breed dogs have no type at all.

The Min Pin's body is compact, slightly wedge-shaped and muscular, with a well-developed forechest.

STYLE

A dog with *style* (sometimes called *elegance*) presents himself well and shows off the breed characteristics that make him typey. He moves with animation, grace, confidence and obvious pride. When two competitors are nearly identical in quality, the more *stylish* one usually wins.

True champions possess the right combination of style, showmanship, soundness, condition, balance, and type.

SHOWMANSHIP

Showmanship is additional flair, combined with timing, boldness and making the most of a fine expression. The ultimate *showman* combines style with showmanship.

The main difference between style and showmanship is that a dog is either born with style or is not. Style can't be taught. Showmanship, on the other hand, can often be helped along. Proper socialization, creative praise and short, interesting practice sessions will teach a dog that showing off is fun and rewarding.

THE AMERICAN KENNEL CLUB STANDARD

The standard already gives a description of the ideal Miniature Pinscher, so why the additional explanations? Because standards are written to guide people who are already familiar with the points of dogs and have some in-depth knowledge of the breed they are studying. That's why new students of the breed often find the terminology in the standard difficult to comprehend. The following explanations should make it easier for you to interpret the standard.

The official AKC standard for the Miniature Pinscher is printed in italics. Explanations and comments on each section follow in regular type.

***General Appearance**—The Miniature Pinscher is structurally a well balanced, sturdy, compact, short-coupled, smooth coated dog. He naturally is well groomed, proud, vigorous and alert. Characteristic traits are his hackney-like*

29

action, fearless animation, complete self-possession, and his spirited presence.

All parts of the Miniature Pinscher are in proportion to each other. A hardy, robust, small dog, he is short in the loin area (the part of the body between the last rib and the pelvis), which gives him a squarish, rather than lanky, look. He has a short straight coat, always appears neat and clean, is constantly aware of his surroundings and moves with haughty, high-stepping aplomb.

Size, Proportion, Substance—Size—10 inches to 12 ¹/₂ inches in height allowed, with desired height 11 inches to 11 ¹/₂ inches measured at highest point of the shoulder blades. Disqualification—Under 10 inches or over 12 ¹/₂ inches in height. Length of males equals height at withers. Females may be slightly longer.

The withers are found just behind the base of the neck and are the top-most part of the dog's shoulder, the highest point on its back. On a male Miniature Pinscher, a measurement from the top of the withers straight down to the ground (height) should equal a measurement from the point of the shoulder to the point of the buttock (length). Any breed of dog where length equals height is referred to as a square breed. Females are allowed to be slightly longer in their body measurement than in their height measurement. Even puppies must be within the size standard to be shown.

Head—In correct proportion to the body. Tapering, narrow with well-fitted but not too prominent foreface which balances with the skull. No indication of coarseness. Eyes— full, slightly oval, clear, bright and dark even to a true black, including eye rims, with the exception of chocolates, whose eye rims should be self-colored. Ears— set high, standing erect from base to tip. May be cropped or uncropped.

Skull— appears flat, tapering forward toward the muzzle. Muzzle— strong rather than fine and delicate, and in proportion to the head as a whole. Head well balanced with only a slight drop to the muzzle, which is parallel to the top of the skull. Nose— black only, with the exception of chocolates which should have a self-colored nose. Lips and Cheeks— small, taut and closely adherent to each other. Teeth— meet in a scissors bite.

The head should not be noticeably large or small, but should be just the right size for the rest of the dog. Another word for foreface is muzzle. It is the area from the tip of the nose to the eyes. Again, balance is important because in order for the Miniature Pinscher to have an attractive head, the foreface and the skull must be in perfect harmony with neither one appearing too long, too short, too wide or too narrow for the other. An excellent Min Pin head could be termed elegant. Coarse heads tend to be short and wide with prominent checks and sometimes a rounded, rather than correctly flat, skull.

Correct eyes are alert and wide opened, not small, squinty, completely round or protruding. Very dark eyes and eye rims are most desirable. Chocolate colored Min Pins will have eye rims the same color as their hair coat.

At conformation shows, dogs are judged against the standard for their breed. This is Ch. Aerborn's Born to Boogie, owned by Paul and Michele Jonas, and shown by Irene Kloeber.

The Miniature Pinscher may be shown with its ears cropped or natural, and is

usually shown cropped in the United States. In either case, placement of the ears should be well up on the skull, enhancing the dog's alert aspect. Low-set ears tend to have tips that point toward ten o'clock and two o'clock, while the correct, high-set ears point toward eleven o'clock and one o'clock.

The muzzle should have depth as well as sufficient width to be in balance with the rest of the head. A good underjaw, or chin, contributes to proper depth. If the jaw is receding or weak and shallow, the muzzle will look pointy and appear longer in profile than it actually is. Undesirably narrow muzzles are often termed "snipy."

Without indication of coarseness, the Miniature Pinscher's skull appears flat, tapering to the muzzle. The neck is slightly arched and gracefully curved.

The slight drop mentioned in the standard is often called a stop in dog terminology. The stop is the indentation just in front of the eyes, between the forehead and the muzzle. Viewed in profile, the stop is evident but

not pronounced, and the skull and muzzle each form a straight line parallel to the other.

Black pigment must completely cover the noses of all Miniature Pinschers, with the exception of chocolates. The self colored noses that chocolates are allowed refers to nose pigment that is the same color as the hair coat.

Black pigment must completely cover the noses of all Miniature Pinschers, with the exception of chocolates. The muzzle should be in balance with the rest of the head.

The tighter the lips fit, the more attractive the muzzle. Pendulous or loose upper lips can spoil the pleasing line of the muzzle by dropping below, and even hiding, the bottom jaw.

Cheeky Miniature Pinschers, those with bulging muscles that give roundness to the cheeks, appear coarse and consequently are not typey.

The incisors are the dog's upper and lower front teeth. In the scissors bite, the lower incisors just touch the inner side of the upper incisors.

Neck, Topline, Body—Neck— proportioned to head and body, slightly arched, gracefully curved, blending into shoulders, muscular and free from suggestion to dewlap or throatiness. Topline—Back level or slightly sloping toward the rear both when standing and gaiting.

Body— compact, slightly wedged shaped, muscular. Forechest well developed. Well-sprung ribs. Depth of brisket, the base line of which is level with points of the elbows. Belly moderately tucked up to denote grace of structural form. Short and strong in loin. Croup level with topline. Tail set high, held erect, docked in proportion to size of dog.

The thickness and length of the neck should coincide with the Miniature Pinscher's head and body. Viewed in profile, a good neck flows smoothly and fluidly into the top of the dog's shoulders (withers). Although not coarse, the neck is well muscled. This is especially noticeable along the top, where the musculature accentuates the slight arch of the neck (sometimes called the crest), which adds to the breed's elegant demeanor. The neck is most narrow just behind the ears and widens gently as it goes downward. At its base, it blends into the withers without any wrinkles.

There should also be no wrinkles on the throat or underside of the neck. Folds of loose skin beginning just under the throat are termed throatiness or as having a dewlap and are not typical of the Miniature Pinscher.

The topline of a dog is the area from the top of the shoulders (withers) to the root of the tail (where the tail meets the body). The correct topline is either parallel to the ground or slightly higher at the withers than at the rump. If it has the slight downward slope, the slant should be a straight line with no curvature. The topline should look the same whether the dog is standing still or moving.

Topline faults to avoid include a roached back, a soft topline, a high rear and wrinkles across the withers. A roached back is a topline where the spine arches in a convex curve that starts behind the withers and becomes pronounced above the loin area. A soft topline, or dip in the topline, is dog show language for a back that sags behind the withers (like a horse that spent years carrying too much weight). High in the rear designates a topline that is higher in the croup than at the withers. This makes a dog look like it is always walking down hill. Wrinkles at the withers are curable if they are caused by obesity, but unfortunately they are more often caused by structural faults in the shoulder blades.

Well-sprung ribs are ribs that make a dog appear well-rounded along the sides, not flat (slab-sided). The ribs need to be spacious and strong as they house and protect the heart and lungs.

A dog will appear compact if his ribs continue quite far back toward his rear quarters. This allows for lung expansion during exertion and may be referred to as either a well-ribbed back or deep in the rear. The gradual tapering back of the ribs gives the slight wedge shape to the body.

A dog's brisket is the area just below his chest, continuing down between the front legs and ending somewhat behind the elbow. It should have enough depth at its lowest point to be even with the dog's elbows.

Think of the top side of the loin as the dog's waistline and the underside as the belly. The entire area should be shapely when you look down on it from above, with a slight indentation at the loin area to keep the body from appearing sausage-like. In profile, the belly angles upward into a shapely waistline, but the area should not be so narrow as to appear weak.

A dog's croup is the area above its hind legs. It's the section of the back that is furthest back, just in front of the root of the tail. The Miniature Pinscher's croup should be in line with the top line, neither higher nor lower.

Tail set refers to the area where the root of the tail and the croup meet. The Min Pin's tail starts high on the croup and is held high. In the United States, the Miniature Pinscher's tail is docked.

Forequarters—Shoulders— clean and sloping with moderate angulation coordinated to permit the hackney-like action. Elbows close to the body. Legs—Strong bone development and small clean joints. As viewed from the front, straight and upstanding. Pasterns strong, perpendicular. Dewclaws should be removed.

Shoulders should be clean and sloping with moderate angulation and elbows close to the body.

Feet— small, cat-like, toes strong, well arched and closely knit with deep pads. Nails thick, blunt.

In a correct front, there is enough room between the front legs to allow for the well-developed chest as it blends downward into the brisket. When the forelegs are too close together, the front is referred to as pinched or tight. Poor angulation of the shoulder blade is often the culprit, as it can cause the chest development to be too slight. This does not mean that more is better in regard to the width of a Miniature Pinscher's chest. As with all other features, balance and proportion are vital. Over-development of the front makes a dog appear coarse and lacking in type and refinement.

The shoulder blade connects the humerus with the vertebrae. The slope of the shoulder blade is usually referred to as layback or angulation, and refers to the angle formed at the joint connecting the shoulder blade (scapula) with the upper arm bone (humerus). In a shoulder with moderate angulation, the scapula slopes backward from its bottom end (at the arm) to its top (just in front of the withers).

When a dog's shoulders lack angulation or layback they are referred to as straight or upright shoulders. In fact, the upper end of the shoulder blade may be so far forward that it is right in the dog's neck. From a practical standpoint, this fault will prevent proper gait by limiting the forward reach of the dog's forelegs. From an aesthetic standpoint, it will make the neck appear too short. To perform the hackney-like gait properly, the Miniature Pinscher must not only be able to high step, but must have reach as well. Moderate angulation allows this, but the 90 degree angulation called for in some other breed's standards would lower the typey high step, just as too little angulation would impede the reach.

Leg bones should be in proportion to the body. This means they should look large enough to easily support the dog's weight. A Miniature Pinscher appears top-heavy if its leg bones have too little circumference, and the term "not enough bone" is used to describe narrow-boned dogs. In addition, the joints should not bulge or protrude.

Seen from the front, the legs should be straight, the elbows should be against the dog's sides (not pointing outward) and the feet should aim straight forward. Feet pointing to the sides (east-west front), feet pointing toward each other (toeing in) or bowed legs are all incorrect.

The pastern is the part of the front leg just above the toes and just under the carpus (wrist joint). Viewed from the front or the side, the pasterns should be straight, erect and perpendicular to the ground. If the pastern bends backward, or allows the feet to turn outward or reach the ground at an angle, the dog may be termed "down in the pasterns." That is just dog language for saying that the pasterns are weak.

You can more easily evaluate your Min Pin against the standard by having him stand on a grooming table.

Your dog's feet should be in proportion to each other and neither splayed nor flat. The Min Pin's hindquarters are well-muscled and, when viewed from the side, well-angulated.

Feet must be in proportion to the dog's size and should not appear too large for the rest of the animal. Space between the toes (splayed feet) and flat feet hamper a dog's endurance and are unattractive. Since the pad cushions the moving dog, it should function as a sturdy running shoe and act as a well padded shock absorber.

Blunt nails are not an inherited trait. Your Min Pin's nails will be blunt if you remember to trim them on a regular schedule.

Hindquarters—*Well muscled quarters set wide enough apart to fit into a properly balanced body. As viewed from the rear, the legs are straight and parallel. From the side, well-angulated. Thighs well muscled. **Stifles**— well defined. Hocks short, set well apart. Dewclaws should be removed. **Feet**— small, catlike, toes strong, well arched and closely knit with deep pads. Nails thick, blunt.*

A dog's rear leg is made up of an upper thigh and a lower thigh, separated by the stifle (knee joint), which is located on

the frontal part of the upper leg. The joint under the lower thigh is called the hock joint. The part of the leg from the hock joint to the foot is commonly called the hock, *The hind legs of the Min Pin have well-muscled thighs capable of strong, driving movement.*
but correctly called the metatarsus or true heel.

In the Miniature Pinscher, the upper and lower thigh should be covered with firm muscle so that the hindquarters appear sturdy and capable of strong, driving movement.

Viewed from the rear, ideal hocks are perfectly straight and parallel to each other. Hocks that turn toward each other (cow hocks) or away from each other (spread or bowed) are undesirable.

Viewed from the side, the leg should make an angle or bend at the stifle joint that coordinates with the angulation of the shoulder blade. Lack of rear angulation in the stifle is termed "straight in the stifle," and is faulty. The practical purpose of rear angulation is that the drive necessary for proper movement comes from flexing and straightening the stifle. Thus, if the stifle is already straight, rear movement will be choppy and unproductive. Poor angulation in either the front or the rear quarter shortens a dog's stride.

Well-defined stifles are stifles with bend (angulation) to them. When a dog has straight stifles, the stifle joints aren't noticeable enough to be considered defined.

Min Pins should have a slightly coarse, closely adhering coat. This pup is being accustomed to grooming at an early age.

Short hocks means that the hocks should not be at mid-point on the leg, but much lower, much closer to the ground. Proper hocks are sometimes referred to as well let down at the hocks. From the side view, the hock should appear low down on the leg and behind, not directly under, the dog's body. From the hock joint down, the lower leg should be perpendicular to the ground.

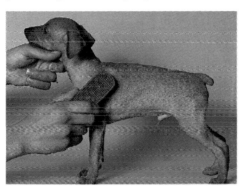

Dewclaws, feet and nails are the same on the rear legs as described for the forelegs.

Coat—Smooth, hard and short, straight and lustrous, closely adhering to and uniformly covering the body.

Hard refers to the coat having a slightly coarse, protective feel instead of a softer velvet-like texture. A closely adhering coat is a healthy one. When the hair sticks out from the skin it is usually due to dryness, and such a coat often lacks luster.

Color—Solid clear red. Stag red (red with intermingling of black hairs). Black with sharply defined rust-red markings on cheeks, lips, lower jaw, throat, twin spots about eyes and chest, lower half of forelegs, inside of hind legs and vent region, lower portion of hocks and feet. Black pencil stripes on toes. Chocolate with rust-red markings the same as specified for blacks, except brown pencil stripes on toes. In the solid red and stag red a rich vibrant medium to dark shade is preferred.

Disqualifications—Any color other than listed. Thumb mark (patch of black hair surrounded by rust on the front of the foreleg between the foot and the wrist; on chocolates, the patch is chocolate hair). White on any part of dog which exceeds one-half inch on its longest dimension.

Red encompasses several shades, from dark fawn to the rich chestnut or mahogany-red of the Irish Setter. Stag reds may come in the same hues as solid reds, and the black hairs intermingled in the red coat are often called guard hairs. The rust-red markings on black and chocolate Min Pins may also vary in hue. To fully understand the thumb print described in the disqualification, look at a Manchester Terrier. Their standard requires the thumb print.

Gait—The forelegs and hind legs move parallel, with feet turning neither in nor out. The hackney-like action is a high-stepping, reaching, free and easy gait in which the front leg moves straight forward and in front of the body and the foot bends at the wrist. The dog drives smoothly and strongly from the rear. The head and tail are carried high.

When front and back legs move parallel, the dog gaits straight forward without side-winding or crabbing, and the front and rear legs do not touch or in any way interfere with each other. Also, the feet do not wing out or turn in.

The Miniature Pinscher's leg action is referred to as hackney-like rather than simply hackney, because those who know horses realize that a hackney pony has little or no rear drive. That type of movement is incorrect in the Min Pin, whose rear legs are expected to drive the body with vigor. What is hackney-like about the movement is that it is desirable for the front legs to be highstepping and bent at the wrist, and to have good reach.

Temperament—Fearless animation, complete self-possession, and spirited presence.

Alert, brave, bright and confident, the King of the Toys presents himself regally.

Disqualifications

Under 10 inches or over 12 ¹/₂ inches in height. Any color other than listed. Thumb mark (patch of black hair *surrounded by rust on the front of the foreleg between the foot and the wrist; on chocolates, the patch is chocolate hair). White on any part of dog which exceeds one-half ($^1/_2$) inch in its longest dimension.*

The AKC standard was approved on July 8, 1980, and reformatted on February 21, 1990.

ADDITIONAL SHOW RING DISQUALIFICATIONS

Besides the specific disqualifications found in the standard for the Miniature Pinscher, the American Kennel Club has some general disqualifications which apply to all breeds.

Spayed and castrated (neutered) animals may not compete in conformation. Dogs that are lame, blind, deaf or missing a testicle, or whose appearance has been changed by artificial means such as plastic surgery, bleach or dye, are also prohibited from competing in the show ring.

Winning Min Pins must combine physical grace and beauty with animated, bright, and confident temperaments.

SELECTING the Right Miniature Pinscher for You

The first step in acquiring a marvelous Miniature Pinscher is finding a first rate breeder. Good breeders are specialists who have spent many years exhibiting and breeding Min Pins and cherish their dogs as a consuming hobby, not as a business. They study dogs and pedigrees in an ongoing effort to select only the best for breeding. That's why they consistently produce fine puppies.

Responsible breeders are concerned about the welfare of their puppies and will probably ask about your past history of dog ownership and why you chose the Miniature Pinscher. They may also ask the ages of your children, how much time you spend at home and if you have a fenced yard. Answer honestly and don't be insulted. The breeder put time, love and money into producing the best possible puppies and wants to make sure that each pup gets a safe and loving home. One way to find Miniature Pinscher breeders is to attend a dog show and talk to the exhibitors after they finish showing. Another way is through the Miniature Pinscher Club of America.

After you have located a few breeders, the next step is contacting them by phone or letter. Make a list of what you want in a puppy and include it in your conversation or letter. Tell the breeder if you want a male or a female, if you have a color preference and what the dog's role will be. For example, will your Min Pin be an all-around family companion, a child's special playmate, a senior citizen's loving lap warmer, a show dog, an obedience trialer, an agility prospect, a therapy dog or any combination of these? Also tell the breeder if you are going to have the dog spayed or neutered, or if you plan to show the dog and breed him at maturity. A complete list of what you want in a Min Pin is especially important if you are purchasing your puppy sight unseen from a distant breeder. Understanding your needs helps the breeder make the right selection for you. If you live within visiting distance of some fine breeders, call for appointments to visit. Most of them will be happy to show you their dogs and answer your questions.

PICK OF THE LITTER

Everyone wants the pick of the litter, but it's not always the same puppy. To the couple with two older children, the pick is the lively puppy with the happy-go-lucky attitude. To the dog show exhibitor, the pick is the puppy that most nearly matches the breed standard. To the elderly woman, the pick is the quiet puppy that will happily snuggle on her lap for hours on end. In truth, the pick is the puppy that appeals to you, provided he has the disposition to fit your lifestyle. Whether you decide to pick your own puppy or ask the breeder to help you choose one, there are many things to take into consideration.

Your idea of the pick of the litter may be completely different than somebody else's. Just be sure that your pick is healthy and has a good temperament.

Attributes of Your Personal Pick Puppy

Did one little Min Pin puppy capture your heart the instant you looked at the litter? Do you keep going back to him even though you want to play with each puppy equally? Are you already naming him in your mind? When the chemistry is that strong, trust it. Just be sure that your special puppy is healthy and has a good temperament.

If there are three or more puppies in the litter, watch them play with each other without human interference. The best pet is usually a puppy in the middle of the pecking order—neither the bully nor the "fraidy cat." A puppy that can back the bully down and then go peacefully about his business deserves special attention.

A healthy puppy's eyes are bright, clear and alert. His coat is glossy and smooth to the touch, and his body should feel surprisingly solid for one so small. The puppy should stand straight on legs that look strong enough to carry his body, and his toes should fit close together and have a nice arch.

Pick up each appealing puppy in turn and cradle him securely in your arms. He may struggle briefly but does he soon relax and enjoy? Does he check you out and try to lick you? These are signs of a good disposition. (When lifting a puppy or an adult Min Pin, always use two hands. Place one hand under his chest and cradle his bottom in your other hand, or place that hand under the loin. Don't let your fingers push your dog's elbows outward or squeeze the front legs together, as this could lead to structural problems. And never, ever lift your Min Pin by the front legs. It's painful and can cause permanent injury to your dog's shoulders. After lifting the dog properly, hold him close to your body. Dogs shouldn't be held dangling in midair.)

Ask permission to take the puppies that appeal to you out of sight of their breeder, dam and littermates so you can see how they react to being alone with you. Do this one puppy at a time and give each one a couple of minutes to survey his surroundings. Then kneel down and encourage him to come to you. Pet him and talk to him when he reaches you, then get up, move away slowly and try to talk him into following you. Next, show the puppy a doggie toy or a small ball. When he seems interested, roll the object slowly away from (not toward) him. Does the puppy follow the toy? You may have to roll the toy three or four times to give the puppy time to figure out the game. Does he eventually examine or chase the toy, or better yet, pick it up in his mouth and carry it?

When the puppy is looking elsewhere, blow a whistle or drop a metal pan about 12 feet away from him. Watch the pup's reaction. It's okay if he was startled, but he should recover quickly.

Even the healthiest pups need frequent naps, so if the Min Pin that caught your eye is too sleepy to play with you, ask the breeder if you may come back for a visit at a different time of day.

If you are purchasing your pup as a potential show dog, check his teeth for a scissors bite (the upper front teeth should meet tightly outside the lower front teeth). Although gait is hard to evaluate in a young pup, watch him move toward and away from you. His front legs should move parallel with each other as the puppy comes toward you and his rear legs should be parallel with each other as he moves away. Show dogs are judged by how closely they conform to the ideal conformation described in the standard.

Even though a puppy is incredibly beautiful, it is important that you are also attracted to his personality. The first few months of puppy ownership are a period of adjustment, but a puppy whose animated attitude makes you smile will make all the adjustments seem minor.

Puppies You Shouldn't Pick

Don't purchase a puppy out of pity. When a litter of playful puppies vies for your attention but one puppy hides in a corner, that puppy is not an abused baby. If the pups were neglected or abused, they would all be fearful. The shy puppy has a

If the pups you want to see are sleeping, take the opportunity to ask the breeder about them and their parents.

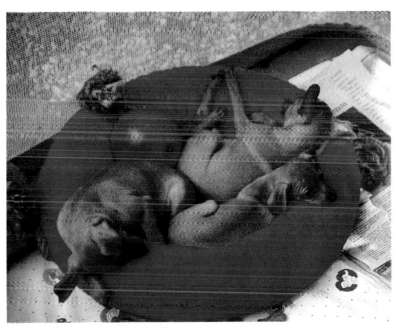

temperament problem. Occasionally it can be reversed, but chances are the shyness is a permanent defect in the puppy's temperament and the dog will never be a confident companion.

Watch the puppies play without human intervention. Do not buy the bully or any puppy that seems to fear his littermates.

Steer clear of skinny puppies as well as puppies with bald patches, diarrhea or mucous seeping from the eyes or nose. Flat, splayed (spread) toes indicate weak feet.

Don't select a puppy that crouches fearfully in one spot or runs away when you take him out of sight of his littermates and breeder. He may need a couple of minutes to get his bearings in a strange place, but he should soon become curious about his surroundings and you.

Pick up a puppy and cradle him close to your body. Is he stiff with fright? Does he struggle or cry? Neither of these reactions are good, but maybe the pup just needs a moment to get used to you. After you caress the puppy, do you feel him gradually relax? If not, the puppy has a poor temperament or was not properly socialized.

SELECTING A MATURE MIN PIN

Min Pin puppies are babies, so they eat sloppily, teethe on everything within reach, "go potty" often and sleep a lot. Nevertheless, they are bright and learn quickly, provided their owners have time to train them and keep them on a regular routine. People who have enough time to enjoy a dog, but do not have the regular schedule necessary to housebreak and care for a puppy, don't have to do

Just as lovable as a puppy, you can also acquire an adult Min Pin. In fact, an adult may be easier for someone who doesn't have the time to housebreak a puppy.

without—not when a mature Min
Pin could brighten their lives.

While not all adult dogs are
housebroken, and unsupervised
young adults may still try to chew
the table legs, mature animals have
bigger bladders and longer
attention spans than puppies, so
they usually learn quite quickly.
Other advantages of acquiring an
adult Min Pin are that you can tell
a great deal about his personality
and see exactly what he looks like.

*Selecting a mature Min
Pin is a bit easier since
you can already see
what he looks like and
tell what type of
personality he has.*

Selecting a mature Min Pin is a
lot like picking a puppy, but
without some of the guesswork.
When checking the disposition of
an adult, take into consideration that mature Min Pins are
discriminating and you are a stranger. If you are on the Min
Pin's home territory, it may take longer for the dog to warm
up to you than if you and the dog were on neutral ground.

Pet and play with the dog to check for a stable
disposition and a willingness to please. Is he happy to
receive your attention or is he fearful or aggressive? It's
important that you and the dog appeal to each other. Does
the sight of the dog make you smile? Is the dog happy to
see you and content in your arms? Ask yourself if you would
like this dog as a constant companion.

To check for general health, look at the dog's skin, eyes,
coat, feet and movement. The skin should be smooth
without bumps, lumps or pimples; the eyes bright and
clear; the coat shiny with no patches of missing hair; the
toes close together and arched; and the movement fluid and
easy. If the dog is lead-broken, ask if you may put a lead on
the dog and take him for a walk. Does he trot along with
you willingly or does he balk, cry, freeze in place or try to
go home?

While a husband can select a Min Pin puppy and bring him
home as a present for his wife (provided she wants a dog), no
family member should receive an adult dog as a surprise.
Something in the dog's past may cause him to be snappish

with women, fearful of men or aloof with children, so every member of the family should meet a grown dog before a decision is made. Finding an adult dog is similar to shopping for a puppy. Attend a dog show if possible to meet breeders, or contact the national Miniature Pinscher Club for a recommendation. The national club also rescues Min Pins in need of new homes.

HEALTH AND MEDICAL RECORDS

When you take your puppy or mature Min Pin home, ask the seller for his feeding, worming and inoculation schedule. Give

Your new puppy shouldn't even leave your home until all of his vaccinations are complete.

the worming and inoculation information to your veterinarian so that the dog's vaccination series can be continued. For your dog's safety, all of his inoculations must be kept up to date. Your new puppy shouldn't even leave your home until his vaccinations are complete. Since inoculation schedules may vary depending on where you live, your veterinarian is the best judge of when your puppy may safely travel with you.

MALE OR FEMALE?

Male and female Miniature Pinschers are equally intelligent, high stepping, alluring, vivacious and loving. While males and females both housebreak in about the same amount of time, sometimes males (if they haven't been neutered) forget their training for a short time just as they become old enough to lift their legs (a sign of sexual maturity). Returning them to the crate training puppy schedule usually resolves the problem in a few days.

SPAYING AND NEUTERING FOR A HEALTHIER, HAPPIER DOG

Dog breeding is an absorbing avocation that combines science, art, commitment and luck, and the only good reason for attempting it at all is a consuming desire to preserve and

Males and females are equally enjoyable and loving. Sex should only be a factor if you decide to breed your dog. If not, it is strongly recommended that you have your dog spayed or neutered. improve the breed. If you have only a casual interest in breeding your female Miniature Pinscher, perhaps to show your children the miracle of birth or to get back your investment, do yourself and your dog a favor and leave breeding to the experts. If something goes wrong during delivery, your children might see their beloved pet die, and even if everything goes right, the puppies could easily cost you more than they earn. Old wives' tales aside, spaying and neutering will not make your dog fat and lazy. Over-feeding and lack of exercise do that. Unless you plan to show your dog in conformation and/or become a dog breeder, the nicest thing you can do for your Min Pin and yourself is to have him spayed or neutered. Females spayed before their first season are at much less risk of developing breast cancer than unspayed females, and they never suffer from infections or cancer of the ovaries or uterus. They also won't bleed for a few days twice a year or add to the unwanted pet problem by having unplanned pregnancies.

Neutering a male dog before he is a year old could save him the pain of prostate problems, including cancer, when he ages. It will also make him easier to live with. Male hormones make dogs desire every female in season whose scent floats past the window, and some of them whine incessantly and try to escape the house or yard to find females. Sometimes these hormones are implicated in housebreaking problems. They also cause frustration, which can make your dog more aggressive toward other dogs and incite him to make love to your mother-in-law's leg during a dinner party. While neutering isn't an instant cure if these problems have become habitual, it starts your dog on the road to improvement by eliminating the production of male hormones.

PEDIGREES

A purebred dog is descended from dogs that were all of the same breed. That means that a purebred Miniature Pinscher's parents, grandparents, great-grandparents and so on were all Miniature Pinschers, as far back as records were kept. The record of a dog's ancestry is called a pedigree, just as the record of a person's ancestry is called a family tree.

Your Min Pin's pedigree may tell you more than just the names of his ancestors. If an ancestor won a title, the abbreviation of the title will appear as part of the dog's name on the pedigree. For example, if an ancestor won his championship competing in conformation shows, the letters Ch. (champion) will appear before his name. If it won an obedience title, such as Companion Dog, the abbreviation CD will appear after his name. But no matter how impressive a pedigree appears, it is only as good as the dog it represents. A great dog with a great pedigree is a treasure, but an inferior dog with a great pedigree is still an inferior dog.

REGISTERING YOUR MINIATURE PINSCHER

When you acquire a puppy or dog represented as registrable, he should come with a registration application that has been filled out and signed by the seller. Your responsibility is to complete the new owner's section of the form and send it to your national kennel club along with the registration fee. They will process your dog's paperwork and send you a registration certificate. Only then is your Min Pin registered.

Sometimes the seller doesn't have a registration application for your new dog. When this occurs, proceed carefully. Perhaps the breeder simply didn't apply soon enough and will have the paperwork in a week or so, but don't buy unless you are very sure. If you are trusting enough to buy anyway, ask for a bill of sale or written statement signed by the seller that includes your new dog's breed, sex, color and date of birth; the registered names and numbers of the puppy's sire and dam; and the name of the breeder. If you don't get your registration application

If you want to register your Min Pin pup, make sure you get the necessary paperwork from the seller.

within a few weeks, write to your national kennel club and identify your puppy by giving all of that information. If you want to buy a registrable Miniature Pinscher and can't get the registration application or every bit of the necessary information, pass up that puppy.

MIN PINS WITH NO PAPERS

If you adopted your Miniature Pinscher from a humane society or a dog rescue group, he probably came without registration papers. That could present a problem if you want to compete in AKC events such as Obedience or Agility. AKC allows purebred dogs with no papers to compete in those events provided they have an ILP (Indefinite Listing Privilege) number. It also helps in the application process if an expert, such as a veterinarian or a respected breeder, writes a note stating that they believe your dog is a purebred Miniature Pinscher.

SEE HOW THEY GROW

Puppies are born blind and deaf, with their eyes and ears tightly

Like all puppies, these Min Pins were born blind and deaf, but they will begin to see and hear around two weeks of age.

shut. Their eyes open when they are between 10 and 15 days old, and their ears start working a few days after that. Baby teeth, which are needle sharp and temporary, emerge at the age of two or three weeks. They are gradually replaced by permanent teeth, starting when the puppies are around four months old. Watch your Min Pin's mouth carefully. If the baby teeth stubbornly remain in place after the permanent teeth begin to emerge, your veterinarian should pull them so the new teeth have room to align properly.

Almost all healthy pups look like champions at six weeks of age, but by three or four months old, some of them begin a gawky adolescence. Your pup may look spindly when he loses his puppy fat. Sections of his body may grow at different rates, making his head look too big or too small, or his chest and rear seem out of balance with each other. Adolescence also brings on behavior changes. When back molars erupt, your well-behaved dog may briefly teethe again. Your outgoing pup may become bashful, and your bright obedience prospect may slow down or even regress in his training.

Even pups go through adolescence, losing puppy fat, which may make them look a bit gangly. They eventually grow out of this stage.

Shyness and stupidity will pass if you patiently ignore them without coddling, sympathizing or becoming annoyed Teething and housebreaking problems (such as marking territory) have to be corrected and your dog confined, just as you taught him manners in the first place. But never fear—your adolescent just needs a brief reminder and he will remember its manners in no time. It often helps to remember that human teens and puppy 'tweens look awkward and act unreasonable just at the age when they are most confused and need the most understanding.

SOCIALIZATION

A dog is socialized when he reacts in a calm and predictable fashion to new people, places and objects. The first human a puppy sees when he opens his tiny eyes to a hazy, out-of-focus world is almost always the breeder or a member of the breeder's family. Next to his dam and littermates, the puppy is most aware of the huge creature who alternately smells of soap, pizza, puppy poo or perfume. Consequently, he will establish his first opinion of what humans are like from his interactions with his two-legged Mom or Dad.

Gentle handling by the breeder is good for even very young Miniature Pinscher puppies, provided the breeder has clean hands and has not been around strange dogs. A few minutes of soft stroking every day gets socialization off to an early start.

Becoming an Individual

It's great fun to sit on the floor and let your developing darlings test their legs by crawling all over you, and it also happens to be good for their mental and physical development. But, aside from the mob scene, each little Min Pin needs his very own few minutes of interaction with you in a different place, away from his littermates. That's when the puppy begins building confidence and developing a personality all his own.

Research by animal behaviorists proves that all puppies go through critical periods of social development from birth to sixteen weeks and that the most vital time of all is between three to seven weeks. If a puppy lacks attention and mental stimulation during that period, his personality won't develop to its full potential. While this sounds scary, it doesn't have to be, because socializing puppies is not only easy, it's fun.

When your puppies are between the ages of three to five weeks, all they need is five or ten minutes alone with a caring

All puppies need some time alone with just you in order to form their own personality. Improper socialization will not allow your dog to reach his full potential.

human at least four times a week. During that time, the human can pet and talk to the puppy or sit on the floor and let the puppy climb all over him. When the puppies reach five weeks old, they need about 15 minutes of individual attention four times a week. It's better if the same person doesn't play with them every

Make time for one-on-one contact between your young puppy and all members of your family.

time. Puppies should learn that men and women, as well as gentle and reliable young people, are all trustworthy. But keep it within the family and close friends. Until your Min Pin pups have been protected by preventative inoculations, they should not be around unfamiliar people or dogs. When you are particularly busy and find it difficult to give the puppies the individual attention they need, simply take one puppy on your lap every time you watch the news or read the paper.

A Stimulating Play Room

A few toys can change your boring puppy room into a stimulating kindergarten. Empty plastic half-gallon milk containers with the caps removed make wonderful playthings. When the puppies gain the courage to examine the bulky objects, they discover that they can dominate the lightweight plastic by dragging it around at will—a wonderful confidence booster. Cardboard boxes with holes cut in strategic places so the puppies can crawl in, out and through are also entertaining. Replace these items when they are soiled or destroyed. Plastic and cardboard are not a good diet, so supervise your demolition dogs if they want to swallow instead of just shake, drag and rip.

To prepare your puppies for a family home, or even for the show ring, it's important that they become accustomed to noise. The best place to begin is with the food dish. Use metal bowls (pie tins are handy) for Min Pin pups that are just learning to lap up semi-solid food and allow the bowls to clang a little instead of laying the tins down carefully. Dry your hair in the puppy room. The small hair-dryer motor is a good prelude to the voluminous vacuum cleaner sounds that send so many Min Pins skittering off in terror. When the puppies are comfortable with the sound of the small motor, gradually vacuum a little closer to their room until they show no more than mild interest.

Easy Does It

The purpose of presenting your pups with various sights, sounds and textures is to familiarize them with the world gradually, not to frighten them. Don't become too creative. Just introduce your litter to ordinary household sights and sounds and keep it simple.

THE NEW OWNER'S ROLE IN SOCIALIZATION

A confident strut is part of the very essence of the Miniature Pinscher, but no dog will behave bravely in strange places unless he is used to going on outings and encountering many different sights and sounds. Dogs form their impressions of the world when they are between 7 and 16 weeks of age. Those nine weeks shape their personalities, making them spirited or shy, fearless or fearful. Socializing puppies is easy and fun, and it is vital that you interact with your puppies frequently. When that critical period of development is over, it can never be recaptured.

When interacting with your Min Pin, remember this guideline—never pet him for being afraid, and always praise him for being brave. When the puppy looks fearful, don't reassure him by cajoling or petting. The puppy will interpret your actions as praise, and panic could become his learned response to the sight of a new person or object. Never yank the puppy toward a feared object either. That type of treatment will turn a little scare into total terror. Instead of encouraging the puppy's fear by babying him or frightening him by using force, just walk up to the new object yourself and touch it like it is a million dollars. Then cheerfully invite the puppy over to share the wonder of it all. If he doesn't buy your act, sit down by the feared object. That will probably entice the pup to crawl over on his belly and eventually examine the scary thing. Once he joins you and examines the object, praise him happily.

Your Min Pin will gain confidence in strange places if he gets out and about as soon as he is safely vaccinated. While safely outside in your arms or on a leash, he will get used to traffic sounds, joggers, shopping carts and people walking strange dogs. Few people can pass by a Min Pin puppy without wanting to pet him, so he will also meet many friendly strangers of all sizes and ages. The more people he meets and the more sights he sees, the more confident he will become, and this will make the world more fun for both of you.

Short car rides are also helpful, as the younger your Min Pin is when he gets used to the motion, the better traveler he will become. These trips will also keep him from associating a ride in the car with going to the veterinary clinic for a vaccination. One ride a week is enough. Soon he will relax and sleep in the car.

After he is vaccinated, take your puppy out and about to introduce him to new sights, sounds, dogs and people. This will get him used to various stimuli.

CARING for Your Miniature Pinscher

Planning ahead for the exciting day when you bring your Miniature Pinscher home will make the transition easier and safer for him and much more fun for you. The amount of food you give your Min Pin and how often you feed him will depend upon his age, activity level and individual metabolism. All dogs need a regular diet with the proper proportions of proteins, carbohydrates, fats, vitamins and minerals.

NUTRITION

Most fine quality commercial dog foods are balanced to provide your Min Pin with optimal nutrition and are far healthier than anything you could create at home for twice the price. The proper balance of vitamins, minerals, fats and proteins is too complicated and too important to guess at, and is better left to the test kitchens of the major dog food companies. Another danger is our human tendency to believe that if a little of something is good for the bones, the appetite or the nerves, then a lot will be even better. This simply isn't true, and, in some cases, more of something may actually be toxic. A good quality commercial food usually contains all the nutrition your Min Pin needs to stay healthy and beautiful. Many dog foods are especially prepared for different stages in dogs' lives and are labeled for puppies, adult dogs and aging dogs.

All dogs must have a well-balanced, nutritious diet, which most high-quality commercial dog foods provide.

Types of Food

Commercial dog foods fall into three major categories: canned, dry and soft-moist. When planning to use only canned food, read the label carefully. Some canned foods provide total nutrition while others are made to be mixed with dry food. If the canned food is meant to be fed alone, it will say something like 100% complete or complete dinner on the label. Some canned dinners are available either chopped or chunky. The nutritional values are equal, but most Miniature Pinschers find it easier to eat the chopped variety.

Don't overfeed your Min Pin. Give him only the proper amount of food to prevent weight problems.

Dry dog foods come in a variety of shapes and sizes. Some are in meal form, with the ingredients simply mixed together. Biscuit food, which may be made up of whole biscuits or crumbled biscuits, is formed by adding flour to the dry ingredients and baking the mixture. Pelleted feed is just meal type food pressed into pellet form. It's important to read the labels because some dry foods are meant to be fed dry, others form gravy when moistened and some may be fed dry or moistened as your Min Pin prefers. Many Min Pins do well on half-dry and half-canned food or two-thirds dry and one-third canned food mixed together.

While convenient and less expensive than the top quality canned foods, most soft-moist foods contain rather high amounts of salt, sugar and preservatives.

Transitions in Feeding

It is never a good idea to suddenly change your dog's diet. When you acquire your Min Pin, ask about his feeding schedule and what brand of dog food he is used to. If you prefer another brand, make the change gradually over the period of a week by adding a bit more of the new brand and taking away a bit more of the old brand each day. This should prevent problems such as diarrhea or constipation.

There is no reason to change dog foods after you find a high quality, well-respected food that your Min Pin enjoys and does well on. Dog foods have eye appeal to attract you, not your dog. Your Min Pin won't get bored with the same food every day like you would, and doesn't need to find new shapes, colors and sizes in his bowl to pique his appetite. As long as you are feeding a high quality food and your Min Pin is thriving, it is unlikely that any change would be for the better.

If the schedule your Min Pin was on before you acquired him is inconvenient for you, go ahead and change it to suit yourself and keep to it as much as possible. Dogs are creatures of habit and they housebreak easiest, function best and remain healthiest on a regular schedule.

Always feed your Min Pin in his own clean bowl and remove it after 10 to 15 minutes, whether all of the food is finished or not. Your Min Pin should have a clean bowl of fresh water available all day. Wash and refill it at feeding time.

You may encounter dog food samples if you purchase dog food or supplies at a feed or pet store, and you will surely be offered samples if you attend dog shows. Try them out if you want to, but never while you and your Min Pin are traveling. Wait until you get him home and settled before offering something new, and then remember to mix it with food he is already used to.

The majority of samples are of more concentrated food than the type generally available at supermarkets. Most of these are excellent feeds that are often used by breeders and exhibitors of show dogs. One reason is that concentrated feed makes for smaller, more compact stools, which makes clean up easier. While this is usually a big plus, an occasional small dog may become constipated from concentrated food. If you try a concentrated food for a few weeks and your Min Pin starts to have problems defecating, gradually go back to what you fed previously. Some small dogs do best on less concentrated feed and stay most regular when eating dog food that contains corn. If your Min Pin is one of them, find a food that keeps his bowels regular and stick with it.

FEEDING A NEW PUPPY

Depending on your Min Pin's age, his breeder probably fed him between three and five times a day. As he gets older, he will eat larger amounts at feeding time, but will need less frequent meals. The total amount of food consumed daily will increase. Most puppies tell you when one of their meals is no longer necessary by showing little interest in food during that feeding for several days in a row.

By the time your Min Pin is three months old, chances are he will be eating three times a day. By six months old, he will be ready for larger amounts twice a day. Although some people feed their dogs once a day after they are a year old, most small dogs, like the Miniature Pinscher, do best on twice-a-day feedings throughout their lives.

Keep your new puppy's feeding schedule consistent with the breeder's. He will eventually eat more at less frequent intervals, but you will be able to tell when to make adjustments.

After your Min Pin is a year old, the two feedings don't have to be equal. For example, the first one may consist of dry food, served dry, which encourages clean gums and teeth, while the second feeding might be a mixture of canned and dry food.

FEEDING AN ADULT MINIATURE PINSCHER

If you are feeding your healthy, parasite-free, adult Miniature Pinscher properly, he will maintain the same weight week after week, be energetic in play, have normal nerves and sport a shiny coat, bright eyes and healthy skin. Careful observation will tell you if there is something missing from your Min Pin's diet, or if he is consuming too many or too few calories. Obesity should be avoided. It is a major health problem in adult dogs and an estimated 41% of the dogs in America are overweight. Avoid table scraps and overfeeding and always give your Min Pin adequate exercise. Obesity is just as hard on dogs as it is on people.

FEEDING THE AGING DOG

Older dogs are best maintained in trim condition but should not be allowed to become too thin. Some dietary adjustments may be needed to help an aging Miniature Pinscher weigh the same as he did in healthy middle age.

Sometimes older dogs have less appetite than they used to and need to be tempted a bit. Warming up the food may be enough to stimulate their hunger. Reverting to puppyhood-style feeding (small amounts at frequent intervals) may also work. A little mashed-up boiled chicken, hard boiled egg or cottage cheese in the food might entice a finicky older pet, but it may spoil the dog so that he expects the same treatment at every meal. But, that's not so terrible. If your Min Pin is suffering some problems associated with advanced age, a little spoiling may make both of you feel better.

Special Circumstances

There are special times in a dog's life when supplementation may be advisable. Bitches in whelp or with nursing puppies may need vitamin and mineral tablets, especially if their appetites are suffering. Show dogs stressed from constantly traveling and competing or dogs recuperating from sickness or an accident may also benefit from dietary supplements. If you think your Min Pin needs a little extra help, check with your veterinarian. He or she may suggest the addition of cottage cheese, hard boiled (never raw) eggs or a little fat to your Min Pin's diet, or put him on a prepared vitamin-mineral powder or tablet.

Avoid These Errors

1. Don't fill up your Miniature Pinscher with table scraps. Little dogs can't hold much food at one time, and no matter how nutritious your dinner is for humans, chances are your Min Pin's food is better for him. Also, dogs that eat table scraps often lose their taste for dog food completely.

2. Don't feed your Miniature Pinscher chocolate or any highly spiced, greasy or salty foods. Chocolate is deadly to some dogs, and spicy sauces and junk food lead to stomach upsets.

3. Don't give your Min Pin any bones other than cooked knuckle bones or Gumabones® by Nylabone®. Chicken, turkey or pork chop bones, for example, can shatter and slice open his intestines with their sharp points.

EXERCISE

The smooth muscles beneath the Min Pin's sleek coat are not the only muscles that are toned and conditioned by regular exercise. His heart is mostly muscle, and even his intestine contains muscle tissue. Blood supply to the muscles is dependent on regular exercise. That means your Min Pin will live longer, be as attractive as possible and behave better if he has sufficient exercise.

Most Min Pins can get enough exercise in a studio apartment if their owners encourage them to play. There are many ways to exercise your Min Pin. Brisk walks are good for both of you, but if you'd rather sit indoors, bring out his balls and other toys and get him involved in a chasing or

To swim or not to swim? Either way, Min Pins love exercising indoors and out.

fetching game. He will also be happy to exercise himself, given a securely fenced yard and a couple of toys. When he is young, your Min Pin will help you discover games that will exercise him. Although he will still need regular exercise when he is older, you may have to initiate it.

GROOMING

Condition your Min Pin from puppyhood to accept grooming as a regular part of life, and he will soon behave well on the grooming table and look forward to the attention. Talk to him softly while you work on him, but if he becomes fidgety about being handled on any part of his body, tell him "no" sharply and firmly and continue grooming. Of course you can sit on the floor and groom your Min Pin, but if you decide to use a table, never, ever leave him on it unattended, not even for a second.

Train your Min Pin to accept grooming and even enjoy it. His good behavior will make grooming that much less of a chore.

Coat and Skin Care

Just a minute or two of daily brushing with a natural bristle brush will keep your Min Pin's skin and coat healthy and shiny. Brushing removes dirt, dead hair, loose skin particles and dandruff, while stimulating circulation and the secretion of natural skin oils.

While brushing your Min Pin, check for ticks and fleas. Ticks are easy to spot on a Miniature Pinscher's sleek coat, but they often hide between the toes, in the ears, in the slightly thicker hair of the neck and just before the tail. To find fleas, rough your Min Pin's coat in the opposite direction from the way it grows. Tiny black specks on the skin are a sign that fleas are present, even if you don't see an actual flea. Ask your veterinarian to recommend an insecticide shampoo or dip, and always use these products exactly as recommended on the label.

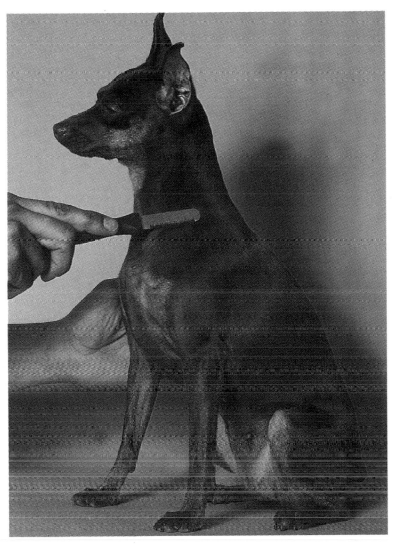

Combing your Min Pin for just a minute or two everyday will keep his skin and coat healthy by removing dirt and dandruff, as well as making it easier to spot fleas and ticks.

Toenails and Teeth

Your Min Pin's toenails are too long if they touch the ground when he is standing still or if they make clicking noises on the floor when he walks. This is uncomfortable and can lead to splayed toes and an unattractive gait.

Clip your Min Pin's toenails if they begin to get too long. Be careful not to cut the quick, as this will hurt and bleed.

To clip your Min Pin's nails, lift his foot up and forward. Then hold it firmly in your left hand so your right hand can do the trimming. (Reverse this if you are left-handed.) When you cut the nail properly, your Min Pin will feel nothing more than slight pressure, the same as you feel when cutting your own toenails. If you accidentally cut the quick (the vein that runs through each nail), your Min Pin's nail will hurt and bleed. Since you won't be able to see the quick in your Min Pin's dark nails, make the cut just outside the hooklike projection on the underside of the nail. Work under good lighting so you can cut your Min Pin's nails without a mishap, but if you accidentally cut the quick (everybody makes an occasional mistake), stop the bleeding with a styptic pencil made for human use or use the styptic powder sold at pet supply stores. Pressing the bleeding nail into a soft bar of soap for a minute or so will also stop the bleeding.

To check your Min Pin's teeth for tartar, hold his head and lift his lips upward. If there are discolorations, use a soft baby toothbrush or the end of a damp washcloth dipped in baking soda. If the stains won't budge, check with your veterinarian. Your Min Pin's teeth may need a professional cleaning.

Bathing

Your Min Pin will seldom need a bath if he is brushed briefly every day. Shampooing washes away the natural oils that moisturize the coat and skin, so bathe him only when necessary.

These pups look well dried after their bath. Make sure to thoroughly rinse off all the shampoo, as any residue can cause severe itching.

Equipment for a bath includes old clothes (when your Min Pin shakes, you'll get wet), a tub (preferably with a drain so he won't be standing in soapy water), a rubber mat for traction in the tub, a spray-nozzle hose attachment or an unbreakable cup for dipping water, pH balanced dog shampoo (or insecticide shampoo or dip if necessary), cotton balls, a washcloth, mineral oil and a towel. Coat conditioner following the shampoo is optional. If you'd rather not bend over, you can bathe your Min Pin in the sink, but don't lose concentration for a second. If he leaps to the floor, he could be severely injured.

Walk your Min Pin outside for a few minutes before beginning his bath. Otherwise he may want to rush outdoors to relieve himself immediately following the bath, and he shouldn't go outside while still damp.

Start by placing part of a cotton ball inside each of your Min Pin's ears to keep the water out. Next, spray or pour water (warm, but not hot) over his whole body with the exception of his face and head. Put a few drops of shampoo on his back and massage the lather into his coat. Add a bit more shampoo as needed to clean his neck, legs, tail and underbelly. If you accidentally get soap in his eyes, relieve the sting by placing a few drops of mineral oil in the inner corner of each eye. When your Min Pin is clean, thoroughly rinse off the lather. Never rush this most important step. When shampoo dries in the coat it can cause intense itching and dull the shine. If you are using insecticide shampoo or dip, follow the label directions carefully.

Wipe your Min Pin's face and head with a warm, well-wrung washcloth. Remove the cotton from his ears and clean each ear gently with a dry cotton ball dipped in a tiny bit of mineral oil. Finish by wrapping him in a towel and towel-drying him well, paying special attention to his chest and underbelly.

PUPPY-PROOFING YOUR HOME

To make your home safe for your Min Pin, put all cleaning agents, antifreeze, pesticides and other household, garage or garden chemicals out of his reach. If you can't eliminate all the electrical wires he can reach, you can coat them with a specially formulated bitter-tasting substance that was created to prevent chewing while being safe for the dog. Since puppies like to play with plants, it is smart to keep them out of your Min Pin's reach, but take extra precautions with poisonous plants as they shed leaves and berries even when they are hanging high. Many common house plants are poisonous, so identify yours and make sure they are non-toxic. Poinsettia leaves, for example, are so dangerous that eating just one can kill a small child, and those pretty mistletoe berries are also deadly poison.

When young and unsupervised, your Min Pin will teethe on everything he can reach, from your shag carpet to your shower curtain, from your briefcase to your bedroom slippers. Hard to handle? Not really. Securing cupboard and closet doors and flipping the shower curtain up over the rod isn't so hard to remember once a precocious Min Pin puppy is part of your family.

From the day you acquire your Min Pin until he is housebroken and stops teething, life will be easiest if you confine him to one easily-cleaned room when there is no one home to supervise him. A bathroom will do, but the kitchen is ideal if it isn't exceptionally large. Use a wire mesh baby gate

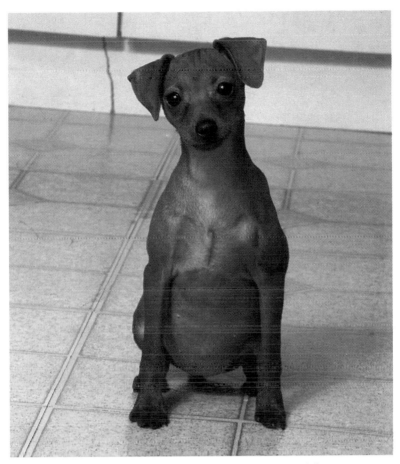

Until your Min Pin is housebroken, it is best to confine him to one easily-cleaned room when no one is home to supervise him. instead of a closed door. That way your Min Pin won't feel punished or banished behind a solid door. If it is impossible to give your Min Pin the run of a room, a baby's playpen with mesh sides is a good alternative.

Using a Crate is Great

Since dogs descended from denning animals that found security in a cozy cave or lair, it will take only a brief period of adjustment before your Min Pin enjoys the comfort and protection of a dog crate. While an occasional new dog owner suspects that crates may be cruel, the exact opposite is true.

In fact, crates have saved dogs' lives and kept dog owners in good moods.

A crate helps tremendously with housebreaking, because your Min Pin will soon learn not to soil his bed. It can double as a safe playpen and is portable enough that you can take it along when you and your Min Pin are traveling. For safety's sake, he should always be crated when riding in a vehicle and the crate should be well secured so it won't slide or roll. A crated dog has a better chance of surviving a car accident than a loose dog does, and you will drive better without your Min Pin jumping all over you.

If it's impossible to give your Min Pin his own puppy-proofed room or even make space for a playpen, you will really appreciate the benefits of a crate. Coming home to a safely crated puppy is much better than coming home to a soiled rug and teeth marks on the table legs.

Your Min Pin's crate should be small enough to be cozy, snug and soft inside. The right size is just large enough so he will be able to stand upright and turn around in it when he is fully grown. Bedding material should be safe if chewed and easy to wash or change in the event of a mishap. For example, several thicknesses of newspaper (black and white, not color like the Sunday comics) make good bedding for a puppy. For extra coziness (Min Pins love having something to burrow under), rip one section into long, thin streamers and place them in the crate on top of the whole sections. Later, when he is crate-broken and finished teething, use a comfortable, washable crate pad.

It's easy to teach your Min Pin to relax in his crate. Every time you put him in it, toss a favorite toy or a special treat in the crate ahead of him. Say "crate," and as gently as possible, place him inside and shut the door. Then leave the area. Don't peer in at him to see how he will react, because that will surely elicit a reaction. Pretty soon, your Min Pin will learn the word crate and enter it himself, without your help.

Never use the crate to punish your Min Pin, and be careful not to use it too much. Your dog should not spend most of his hours in a crate. As he matures, his attitude toward his crate should become neutral. If he loves it so much that it's hard to get him to leave it, or if he hates it, something is wrong. When your Min Pin is grown and house trained, you may still want to leave a crate in a corner with its door always open. Your Min Pin will appreciate a hideaway of his own where he can take a nap when he needs one. Children can be taught that he retires to his crate when he is tired and should be left alone.

Your Min Pin may cry the first few times he is introduced to his crate, but if you walk away and don't take him out of the crate until he settles down, he'll soon become accustomed to it. No matter how much noise he makes, tough it out. Never take him out of the crate to stop the racket. That's exactly what he wants and it will teach him that loud complaints are rewarded. Wait until he is silent for at least a minute before going to him and letting him out.

PUPPY EQUIPMENT

Safe Toys

Your Min Pin needs something safe to gnaw on while he is teething and should have a toy or two available all the time. Whenever he is placed in his crate, he should be accompanied by a safe toy. Toys should also be handy when he is out and about, enjoying the family. Although your Min Pin will continue chewing when he grows up, he won't gnaw on everything in sight the way teething puppies do. Chewing is good for adult dogs

These Min Pins love their Gumabones®. Since all dogs chew by nature, it is best to give them safe and acceptable devices, so they don't choose your furniture.

71

as it promotes healthy gums and helps keep the teeth clean.

Rawhide chew toys are a traditional favorite, but there have been rare incidents when a dog choked from getting a bit of rawhide caught in his throat. It's fine to give your Min Pin rawhide when you are home and in the same room with him, but don't choose rawhide for his crate toy. The safe alternative to rawhide is Roar-Hide™. It is cut up, melted and molded into a dog bone shape that won't break into harmful pieces.

Your Min Pin will surely enjoy a squeaky toy (lightweight rubber or plastic figure with a squeaker inside). However, these toys tear easily and can be swallowed, dangerous squeaker and all. Even when you aren't home, he can safely play with a chew toy made of hard nylon, like the ones made by Nylabone®, or the softer polyurethane toys, called Gumabones®.

Nylafloss®, the braided nylon rope toys sold at pet supply stores, are fun for games of tug of war, and good for helping to keep your Min Pin's teeth tartar free. Providing your dog with safe chew toys should keep him busy for quite awhile.

Dog Dishes

Good dog dishes are easy to clean and are shaped or weighted so they won't tip over. Your Min Pin should have one for food and another for water. The food dish should be washed after each use, and the water dish should be refilled with fresh water frequently and washed thoroughly once a day. When purchasing dishes, remember that your Min Pin will grow a little and so will the size of his meals.

Grooming Equipment

A wash-n'-wear breed, Miniature Pinschers need only a little grooming to absolutely glow. All you need to keep yours beautiful are a brush with short, soft to medium bristles or a hound glove (a mitten with natural bristles); a toenail clipper; pH balanced dog shampoo (sometimes you may need insecticide shampoo or dip) and a soft toothbrush. Additional bathing and grooming needs are probably already in your medicine chest.

Collar and Leash

Take your Min Pin with you when buying his collar and choose one that applies no pressure as it encircles his neck, but isn't loose enough to slip over his head. The collar should be flat, made of nylon webbing or leather, with a small buckle and ring for attaching the lead. Check the fit of the collar frequently. Puppies grow fast, and collars must be replaced immediately when they become too small. Your Min Pin's lead should be four to six feet long and made of a flexible fabric such as leather or nylon.

Min Pins are a relatively low-maintenance breed when it comes to grooming. They really only need regular brushing or combing, as well as a toenail clipping when necessary.

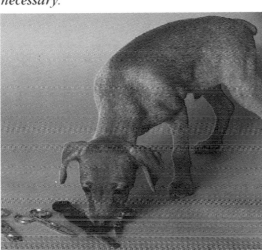

Poop Scoop

Poop scoops are convenient for cleaning up your yard and for cleaning up after your Min Pin when you take him for walks. While an array of items are available for this purpose, many owners of small dogs just carry a couple of plastic bags in their pocket or purse. These may be turned inside out for a quick pick-up, then closed and tossed in the nearest garbage can.

Cleaning Chores

Your Min Pin's food and water dishes must be kept clean to prevent the growth of disease-producing bacteria. If he has an outdoor play area, scoop it frequently. This will help control worms and biting insects.

Prevention pays when taking care of a Miniature Pinscher. This is a happy, healthy and hardy breed, and a little common sense will keep your perky pup in top form.

HOUSEBREAKING and Training

Your Min Pin may tickle you with his vibrant attitude, and parade on lead like a born performer, but if he lacks house manners, he isn't the pure pleasure he could be. Don't let his small size fool you. For all his cuteness, your Min Pin is a highly intelligent dog. He is also highly trainable and capable of learning everything that you are capable of teaching him.

HOUSEBREAKING

Successful housebreaking results from a regular routine and an alert trainer. A housebroken dog is simply a dog with a habit—the happy habit of eliminating outdoors.

Miniature Pinschers are basically clean dogs, and try not to eliminate where they eat or sleep. Using this fact can help you train your Min Pin. When housebreaking, confine him to a small, safe area, such as a dog crate, or one easily cleaned room of the house (such as the kitchen or bathroom) every time you are away or he is unsupervised. When you get home, take him outside immediately and fuss over him with happy praise when he eliminates. If your Min Pin already soiled his crate or playroom, take him outside anyway and clean up the mess right away. Besides being dangerous to his health, making your Min Pin stay in a wet or dirty crate teaches him to live with his mess, and that slows down the housebreaking process. If you have to be away for several hours at a time, use a room rather than a crate. Your young Min Pin has to relieve himself often, and should never be forced into filthy living.

Your Min Pin must be on a regular feeding and watering schedule for housebreaking to be successful. Take him outside first thing in the morning and praise him for a job well done. Young pups need to relieve themselves right after they eat, so after he has breakfast and a drink, take him outside again. Then remember to confine him to his comfortable crate or play area (with a safe toy or two) when you leave the house, or even when you are home but unable to watch him.

By lunch time, he will have to repeat the cycle. Take him outdoors as soon as he is removed from the confined area. Then give him food and water and take him outdoors again.

Make time to enjoy your Min Pin in the evening. Take him outdoors as soon as you arrive home, praise him for eliminating, and if the weather is nice, have some fun with him. Then let him join you in the kitchen while you cook dinner and let him warm your lap during the evening news. Until he is mature and reliably housebroken, your Min Pin should receive his last meal of the day between 6:00 and 7:00 p.m. Even his water bowl should disappear until morning. When he finishes eating, take him outside, praise him, and enjoy each other for the rest of the evening. Just before you go to bed take him outside again. Then confine him safely for the night.

Housebreaking your puppy is relatively easy if you put him on a regular schedule. Always take him to the same spot, and praise him when he does what he should.

HELPFUL HOUSEBREAKING HINTS

All dogs are different and your Min Pin may have to relieve himself more or less often than this schedule anticipates.

Puppies give clues about their intentions, so watch him closely. Take him outside if he begins walking in circles and sniffing the floor, starts panting when he hasn't been exercising, or suddenly leaves the room. Puppies almost always have to relieve themselves after play periods or exercise, so a trip outdoors when play is over is always a good idea. Preventing mistakes usually results in a housebroken dog while corrections often lead to worse problems. Expect mistakes and don't get upset by them. Your puppy is young, and will have to learn control slowly, just as human babies do. When you come home to a soiled crate, hold your temper. He won't remember what he did, so he won't understand why you are yelling at him when he was so happy to see you. That type of misunderstanding is more serious than a simple housebreaking setback. If he already relieved himself, take him outside anyway and use an odor neutralizer or plain

Watch for signs that your Min Pin needs to relieve himself. Walking in circles and sniffing the ground usually mean that he needs to go.

If the snow drifts are too high for your Min Pin, it may be better to paper train him. white vinegar when cleaning up the soiled spot. Never use anything containing ammonia to clean up after your Min Pin. The smell makes some dogs seek out the same spot to go potty again.

Catching your Min Pin in the act is different than coming home and finding a mess. If you see him getting into position, you may be able to stop him mid-squat with a loud noise, like clapping your hands or stamping your foot. Then pick him up, hurry him outside, and praise him for finishing what he started. Don't use the outdated method of spanking him with a rolled up newspaper or rubbing his nose in his mess. Such punishments teach him to hide from you and eliminate behind the sofa where he thinks you won't find it, instead of performing proudly for praise.

PAPER TRAINING

If the snow drifts in your yard are higher than a Min Pin's ear, or if you are away several hours a day, or live on the 18th floor of a city apartment, you may prefer paper training. Use an uncarpeted room close to family activity (such as the kitchen) and cover the entire floor with several thicknesses of newspaper (prevail upon neighbors and friends to save you their papers for a couple of weeks). Put your Min Pin in this area whenever you are unable to watch him. When you get home, clean up the results by simply throwing away the soiled papers. Don't throw away the bottom paper, though. It will have just enough scent on it to entice him to use the same spot again. Instead, make the bottom paper the new top paper, and put clean papers under it. Soon your Min Pin will relieve himself in his chosen spot every time you aren't around to take him outside, and you can gradually reduce the amount of floor you cover with paper. Just don't make it too small, as his aim could be slightly off.

Once your Min Pin eliminates in the same small spot regularly, you can begin moving the paper a few inches closer to the door each day. Don't rush this step, and be sure to continue using the previous bottom paper as the new top paper. Eventually his paper will be right at the door and your Min Pin will have the habit of going to the door when he needs to relieve himself.

NOISE CONTROL

Most puppies sing a lonesome song when their family confines them. There are several ways to control the cacophony, so try the least forceful method first and move up from there. With any of these methods, don't stand around waiting to see your Min Pin's reaction to confinement and solitude, as that will elicit a reaction for sure. Never take him out of his place of confinement to stop his racket. That's exactly what he wants, so he will feel rewarded for complaining loudly. Wait until he is silent for at least a minute before going to him and letting him out.

Despite their harmless appearance, all new puppies will make a mess before they are properly housebroken. However, you should only correct your Min Pin if you catch him in the act.

With no audience, your Min Pins may begin to cry, but don't give in or they will feel rewarded for complaining.

Always keep in mind that your Min Pin isn't being confined as punishment, but as a convenience to you—to help you housebreak him and keep your home intact during the period of adjustment. Eventually he should begin to think of his confinement area as his very own space within your home, so make him happy there. Be sure he always has a soft place to nap, an interesting toy or two and fresh water. Then put him in his own area when you need to, and walk away without looking back. To quiet him, try these methods in the following order:

1. The first few times you confine him and leave him alone, just put up with the noise for ten minutes without doing anything. Some puppies simply stop singing when there is no audience.

2. Play a radio softly to help him relax, but keep the cord and the radio out of his reach.

3. If a week of adjustment and a radio don't help, make a sudden sharp noise from another room, such as banging two pans together or stamping your foot. Don't say anything, however, since you want your Min Pin to think that his barking, not you, caused the scary sound. As soon as he makes noise again, make the reprisal racket. Repeat as often as necessary.

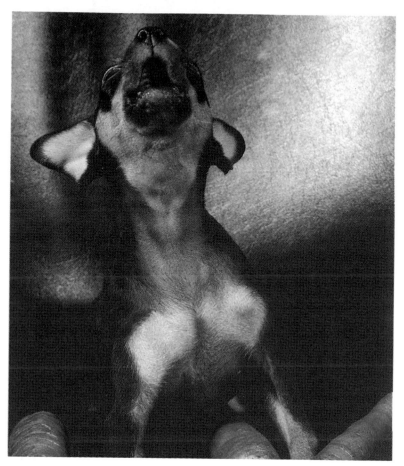

The first few times you leave your pup alone, just put up with his crying for ten minutes or so.

4. Fill a small, inexpensive (not powerful) water pistol. When your Min Pin barks or whines, walk in silently and squirt him one time, straight in the face. Then leave again. When he is quiet for a little while, go to him happily without the water pistol and praise him. Repeat as necessary.

Give him enough attention so he feels loved and secure, and don't feel guilty about leaving him safely confined until he learns house manners. If you praise everything he does right, and never reward noise tantrums or fear reactions, your Min Pin will be a joy all his life.

LEAD-BREAKING YOUR MIN PIN PUPPY

The best collar for lead breaking your Min Pin is a round or flat leather buckle collar or a nylon buckle collar. The buckle should be small and lightweight so it doesn't weigh down your little dog. Use the buckle collar instead of a show lead even if you plan to show your Min Pin. While they are teething, puppies often have swollen glands on either side of the throat. These can become quite sensitive, and a show lead puts pressure on that area and intensifies the soreness. After his permanent teeth erupt and the pain is gone, he will easily learn how to gait on a show lead if he is already lead broken.

Sometimes you might feel it's easier to just carry your Min Pin around .

Allow him to get used to his collar first and then add his lead. Put the collar on him for the first time just before you feed him and let him eat while wearing it. He should wear it a little longer each day for three or more days, or

until he stops scratching at it every few seconds. Then introduce the lead by attaching it to the collar and letting him drag it around. Never leave the room while the lead is dangling, as it could become caught on something.

After he seems relaxed with the collar and lead, take him to some wide open spaces (or a large indoor area). Hold your end of the lead, and allow him to take you for a walk. Do this two or three times before introducing him to an immovable object.

A door knob makes a fine immovable object, provided the door is tightly shut and no one will be using it for the next five minutes. Attach your end of the lead to the knob and then ignore him, but stay in the room and watch TV or read a book. He may fight the lead and scream, but as long as there is nothing nearby for him to become tangled in, he should be fine. He's going to stage a freedom fight the first time he feels lead pressure anyway, and it's better if he argues with a solid object rather than you. Hook your Min Pin up to the object once or twice a day, for two or three days, and he will soon get over his indignation and learn how to relieve the pressure on his collar. When he has made peace with his lead, he's ready to go back outside (or to a large indoor area), with you holding the lead again.

Let your Min Pin lead you just to start him moving happily, then choose the direction you want to go and exert soft pressure on the lead to encourage him to walk with you. During the early stages it works best if you walk him toward a familiar place. For example, you could carry him a quarter block down the street, then put him down and walk him toward home. As he prances along, praise him happily. Don't worry about his position as long as he is going with

Five to ten minutes of lead training a day is enough early on. Continually praise him as he gets used to not only the lead, but your leadership.

Introduce your Min Pin to the grooming table as soon as possible and make it a pleasant and safe experience. you rather than balking or trying to take you somewhere else. He might lag behind a little, or pull ahead or slightly sideways, but that's fine this early in training. Between five and ten minutes of daily practice on lead is enough, and more than that is too much. Soon he will be accustomed to his lead and your leadership, and will enjoy exploring unfamiliar territory with you. When walking him no longer feels like a training session, you can enjoy nice long walks together. Isn't it convenient that your Min Pin is tiny? If he gets tired you can carry him home.

TAMING TABLE TERROR

If you are planning a show career for your Min Pin, or just want to save your back by putting him on a table for grooming, introduce him to the table as soon as you get him and make the experience pleasant and safe. Use a table made especially for grooming dogs, or any sturdy, steady table with a non-slip surface. Always watch him carefully to avoid a disastrous fall.

As soon as you place him on the table, pet and praise him. Use tickling and happy talk to get his tail twitching, and even if he seems to be having fun, praise him and quit after three minutes. It's okay to practice as often as three times a day, as long as you observe the three minute limit. If over two minutes go by and you have not been able to convince him to relax and enjoy himself, praise him anyway

The proper mix of praise, patience, and a sense of humor will enable you to easily train your Min Pin.

and remove him from the table. Next time put him up there when you are sure he is hungry and give him treats. Once he is relaxed on the table, he can stay on it long enough to be groomed. If the phone rings though, don't turn away with him on the table. Pick up your little friend and take him with you.

CANINE-ASSISTED THERAPY

Would you like to share your Min Pin's love of life with someone who needs a little cheer? Well-trained therapy dogs bring rays of sunshine to residents of nursing homes, hospices, children's wards and other institutions. Therapy dogs need special attributes. They have to be obedient and totally confident, with an outgoing personality. In addition they should be comfortable around new sounds, sights and

medicinal smells, while accomplishing their mission of turning strangers into friends. At least three national organizations, Therapy Dogs International, Delta Society and Therapy Dogs Incorporated have certification programs and tests for potential therapy dogs. For information contact Therapy Dogs International (201) 543-0888; Delta Society (206) 226-7357; or Therapy Dogs Incorporated, P.O. Box 2796, Cheyenne, WY 82003.

The Min Pin's confident, friendly demeanor makes him a great candidate for a therapy dog.

SPORT of Purebred Dogs

Welcome to the exciting and sometimes frustrating sport of dogs. No doubt you are trying to learn more about dogs or you wouldn't be deep into this book. This section covers the basics that may entice you, further your knowledge and help you to understand the dog world. If you decide to give showing, obedience or any other dog activities a try, then I suggest you seek further help from the appropriate source.

These three beautiful Min Pins look like they are ready for any challenge thrown their way.

Dog showing has been a very popular sport for a long time and has been taken quite seriously by some. Others only enjoy it as a hobby.

Easy Does It Drum N' Up, owned by Bobbie Crissey, clears the bar jump during obedience training.

The Kennel Club in England was formed in 1859, the American Kennel Club was established in 1884 and the Canadian Kennel Club was formed in 1888. The purpose of these clubs was to register purebred dogs and maintain their Stud Books. In the beginning, the concept of registering dogs was not readily accepted. More than 36 million dogs have been enrolled in the AKC Stud Book since its inception in 1888. Presently the kennel clubs not only register dogs but adopt and enforce rules and regulations governing dog shows, obedience trials and field trials. Over the years they have fostered and encouraged interest in the health and welfare of the purebred dog. They routinely donate funds to veterinary research for study of genetic disorders.

Following are the addresses of the kennel clubs in the United States, Great Britain and Canada.

The American Kennel Club
51 Madison Avenue
New York, NY 10010
(Their registry is located at: 5580 Centerview Drive, STE 200,
Raleigh, NC 27606-3390)

The Kennel Club
1 Clarges Street
Piccadilly, London, WIY 8AB, England

The Canadian Kennel Club
111 Eglinton Avenue
East Toronto, Ontario M6S 4V7
Canada

Today there are numerous activities that are enjoyable for both the dog and the handler. Some of the activities include conformation showing, obedience competition, tracking, agility, the Canine Good Citizen Certificate, and a wide range of instinct tests that vary from breed to breed. Where you start depends upon your goals, which may not be immediately apparent.

Puppy kindergarten will provide a basic obedience and socialization foundation for your rambunctious new Min Pin.

PUPPY KINDERGARTEN

Every puppy will benefit from this class. PKT is the foundation for all future dog activities from conformation to "couch potato." Pet owners should make an effort to attend even if they never expect to show their dog. The class is designed for puppies about three months of age with graduation at approximately five months of age. All the puppies will be in the same age group and, even though some

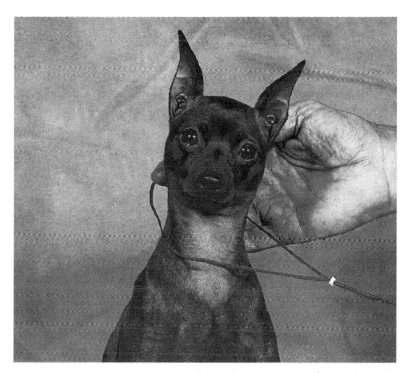

All Min Pins should learn the basic commands of sit, stay, heel, down, and come.

may be a little unruly, there should not be any real problem. This class will teach the puppy some beginning obedience. As in all obedience classes the owner learns how to train his own dog. The PKT class gives the puppy the opportunity to interact with other puppies in the same age group and exposes him to strangers, which is very important. Some dogs grow up with behavior problems, one of them being fear of strangers. As you can see, there can be much to gain from this class.

There are some basic obedience exercises that every dog should learn. Some of these can be started with puppy kindergarten.

Sit

One way of teaching the sit is to have your dog on your left side with the leash in your right hand, close to the collar. Pull up on the leash and at the same time reach

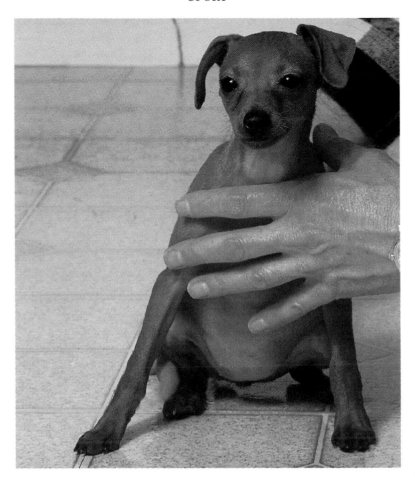

Teaching your dog to sit can be easily done by saying his name, followed by the command, and gently guiding him into the seated position.

around his hindlegs with your left hand and tuck them in. As you are doing this say, "Beau, sit." Always use the dog's name when you give an active command. Some owners like to use a treat, holding it over the dog's head. The dog will need to sit to get the treat. Encourage the dog to hold the sit for a few seconds, which will eventually be the beginning of the Sit/Stay. Depending on how cooperative he is, you can rub him under the chin or stroke his back. It is a good time to establish eye contact.

Down

Sit the dog on your left side and kneel down beside him with the leash in your right hand. Reach over him with your left hand and grasp his left foreleg. With your right hand, take his right foreleg and pull his legs forward while you say, "Beau, down." If he tries to get up, lean on his shoulder to encourage him to stay down. It will relax your dog if you stroke his back while he is down. Try to encourage him to stay down for a few seconds as preparation for the Down/Stay.

Lavish praise and an occasional treat are good ways to stimulate and reinforce positive behavior when teaching basic commands.

Heel

The definition of heeling is the dog walking under control at your left heel. Your puppy will learn controlled walking in the puppy kindergarten class, which will eventually lead to heeling. The command is "Beau, heel," and you start off briskly with your left foot. Your leash is in your right hand and your left hand is holding it about half way down. Your left hand should be able to control the leash and there should be a little slack in it. You want him to walk with you with your leg somewhere between his nose and his shoulder. You need to encourage him to stay with you, not forging (in front of you) or lagging behind you. It is best to keep him on a fairly short lead. Do not allow the lead to become tight. It is far better to give him a little jerk when necessary and remind him to heel. When you come to a halt, be prepared physically to make him sit. It takes practice to become coordinated. There are excellent books on training that you may wish to purchase. Your instructor should be able to recommend one for you.

Come

This quite possibly is the most important exercise you will ever teach. It should be a pleasant experience. The puppy may learn to do random recalls while being attached to a long line such as a clothes line. Later the exercise will start with the dog sitting and staying until called. The command is "Beau, come." Let your command be happy. You want your dog to come willingly and faithfully. The recall could save his life if he sneaks out the door. In practicing the recall, let him jump on you or touch you before you reach for him. If he is shy, then kneel down to his level. Reaching for the insecure dog could frighten him, and he may not be willing to come again in the future. Lots of praise and a treat would be in order whenever you do a recall. Under no circumstances should you ever correct your dog when he has come to you. Later in formal obedience your dog will be required to sit in front of you after recalling and then go to heel position.

CONFORMATION

Conformation showing is our oldest dog show sport. This type of showing is based on the dog's appearance—that is his structure, movement and attitude. When considering this type of showing, you need to be aware of your breed's standard and be able to evaluate your dog compared to that standard. The breeder of your puppy or other experienced breeders would be good sources for such an evaluation. Puppies can go through lots of changes over a period of time. I always say most puppies start out as promising hopefuls and then after maturing may be disappointing as show candidates. Even so this should not deter them from being excellent pets.

Conformation is our oldest dog sport. It is based on the dog's appearance—his structure, movement, and attitude.

Usually conformation training classes are offered by the local kennel or obedience clubs. These are excellent places for training puppies. The puppy should be able to walk on a lead before entering such a class. Proper ring procedure and technique for posing (stacking) the dog will be demonstrated as well as

It takes time to learn the fine art of conformation showing. These are all experienced handlers.

gaiting the dog. Usually certain patterns are used in the ring such as the triangle or the "L." Conformation class, like the PKT class, will give your youngster the opportunity to socialize with different breeds of dogs and humans too.

It takes some time to learn the routine of conformation showing. Usually one starts at the puppy matches which may be AKC Sanctioned or Fun Matches. These matches are generally for puppies from two or three months to a year old, and there may be classes for the adult over the age of 12 months. Similar to point shows, the classes are divided by sex and after completion of the classes in that breed or variety, the class winners compete for Best of Breed or Variety. The winner goes on to compete in the Group and the Group winners compete for Best in Match. No championship points are awarded for match wins.

A few matches can be great training for puppies even though there is no intention to go on showing. Matches enable the puppy to meet new people and be handled by a stranger—the judge. It is also a change of environment, which broadens the horizon for both dog and handler. Matches and other dog activities boost the confidence of the handler and especially the younger handlers.

Earning an AKC championship is built on a point system, which is different from Great Britain. To become an AKC Champion of Record the dog must earn 15 points. The number of points earned each time depends upon the number of dogs in competition. The number of points available at each show depends upon the breed, its sex and the location of the show. The United States is divided into ten AKC zones. Each zone has its own set of points. The purpose of the zones is to try to

equalize the points available from breed to breed and area to area. The AKC adjusts the point scale annually.

The number of points that can be won at a show are between one and five. Three-, four- and five-point wins are considered majors. Not only does the dog need 15 points won under three different judges, but those points must include two majors under two different judges. Canada also works on a point system but majors are not required.

Dogs always show before bitches. The classes available to those seeking points are: Puppy (which may be divided into 6 to 9 months and 9 to 12 months); 12 to 18 months; Novice; Bred-by-Exhibitor; American-bred; and Open. The class winners of the same sex of each breed or variety compete against each other for Winners Dog and Winners Bitch. A Reserve Winners Dog and Reserve Winners Bitch are also awarded but do not carry any points unless the Winners win is disallowed by AKC. The Winners Dog and Bitch compete with the specials (those dogs that have attained championship) for Best of Breed or Variety, Best of Winners

To become an AKC Champion of Record, a dog must earn 15 points under three different judges. Standards in England are a bit different, with dogs having to earn three Challenge Certificates.

and Best of Opposite Sex. It is possible to pick up an extra point or even a major if the points are higher for the defeated winner than those of Best of Winners. The latter would get the higher total from the defeated winner.

At an all-breed show, each Best of Breed or Variety winner will go on to his respective Group and then the Group winners will compete against each other for Best in Show. There are seven Groups: Sporting, Hounds, Working, Terriers, Toys, Non-Sporting and Herding. Obviously there are no Groups at specialty shows (those shows that have only one breed or a show such as the American Spaniel Club's show, which is for all flushing spaniel breeds).

This talented Min Pin can't wait to show off why he is called the "King of Toys."

Earning a championship in England is somewhat different since they do not have a point system. Challenge Certificates are awarded if the judge feels the dog is deserving regardless of the number of dogs in competition. A dog must earn three Challenge Certificates under three different judges, with at least one of these Certificates being won after the age of 12 months. Competition is very strong and entries may be higher than they are in the U.S. The Kennel Club's Challenge Certificates are only available at Championship Shows.

In England, The Kennel Club regulations require that certain dogs, Border Collies and Gundog breeds, qualify in a working capacity (i.e., obedience or field trials) before becoming a full Champion. If they do not qualify in the working aspect, then they are designated a Show Champion, which is equivalent to the AKC's Champion of Record. A Gundog may be granted the title of Field Trial Champion (FT Ch.) if it passes all the tests in the field but would also have to qualify in conformation before becoming a full Champion. A Border Collie that earns the title of Obedience Champion (Ob Ch.) must also qualify in the conformation ring before becoming a Champion.

English regulations require that a dog qualify in a working capacity before becoming a full champion, a major difference from the American system.

The U.S. doesn't have a designation full Champion but does award for Dual and Triple Champions. The Dual Champion must be a Champion of Record, and either Champion Tracker, Herding Champion, Obedience Trial Champion or Field Champion. Any dog that has been awarded the titles of Champion of Record, and any two of the following: Champion Tracker, Herding Champion, Obedience Trial Champion or Field Champion, may be designated as a Triple Champion.

The shows in England seem to put more emphasis on breeder judges than those in the U.S. There is much competition within the breeds. Therefore the quality of the individual breeds should be very good. In the United States we tend to have more "all around judges" (those that judge multiple breeds) and use the breeder judges at the specialty shows. Breeder judges are more familiar with their own breed since they are actively breeding that breed or did so at one time. Americans emphasize Group and Best in Show wins and promote them accordingly.

Although the Min Pin's tail is customarily docked, one with a natural tail is not disqualified from the show ring.

It is my understanding that the shows in England can be very large and extend over several days, with the Groups being scheduled on different days. I believe there is only one all-breed show in the U.S. that extends over two days, the Westminster Kennel Club Show. In our country we have cluster shows, where several different clubs will use the same show site over consecutive days.

Westminster Kennel Club is our most prestigious show although the entry is limited to 2500. In recent years, entry has been limited to Champions. This show is more formal than the majority of the shows with the judges wearing formal attire and the handlers fashionably dressed. In most instances the quality of the dogs is superb. After all, it is a show of Champions. It is a good show to study the AKC registered breeds and is by far the most exciting especially since it is televised! WKC is one of the few shows in this country that is still benched. This means the dog must be in his benched area during the show hours except when he is being groomed, in the ring, or being exercised.

Typically, the handlers are very particular about their appearances. They are careful not to wear something that will detract from their dog but will perhaps enhance it. American ring procedure is quite formal compared to that of other countries. I remember being reprimanded by a judge because I made a suggestion to a friend holding my second dog outside the ring. I certainly could have used more discretion so I would not call attention to myself. There is a certain etiquette expected between the judge and exhibitor and among the other exhibitors. Of course it is not always the case but the judge is supposed to be polite, not engaging in small talk or even acknowledging that he knows the handler. I understand that there is a more informal and relaxed atmosphere at the shows in other countries. For instance, the dress code is more casual. I can see where this might be more fun for the exhibitor and especially for the novice. This country is very handler-oriented in many of the breeds. It is true, in most instances, that the experienced professional handler can present the dog better and will have a feel for what a judge likes.

In England, Crufts is The Kennel Club's own show and is most assuredly the largest dog show in the world. They've been known to have an entry of nearly 20,000, and the show lasts four days. Entry is only gained by qualifying through

The Westminster Kennel Club Dog Show is the most prestigious in the United States. It is held annually in New York City.

winning in specified classes at another Championship Show. Westminster is strictly conformation, but Crufts exhibitors and spectators enjoy not only conformation but obedience, agility and a multitude of exhibitions as well. Obedience was admitted in 1957 and agility in 1983.

The Crufts Dog Show is England's most prestigious show, with entries numbering near 20,000 dogs in a variety of events including agility, pictured here.

If you are handling your own dog, please give some consideration to your apparel. For sure the dress code at matches is more informal than the

This is Champion Seville In Tempo With Madric, Best in Breed winner at the 1994 Westminster Kennel Club Show.

point shows. However, you should wear something a little more appropriate than beach attire or ragged jeans and bare feet. If you check out the handlers and see what is presently fashionable, you'll catch on. Men usually dress with a shirt and tie and a nice sports coat. Whether you are male or female, you will want to wear comfortable clothes and shoes. You need to be able to run with your dog and you certainly don't want to take a chance of falling and hurting yourself. Heaven forbid, if nothing else, you'll upset your dog. Women usually wear a dress or two-piece outfit, preferably with pockets to carry bait, comb, brush, etc. In this case men are the lucky ones with all their pockets. Ladies, think about where your dress will be if you need to kneel on the floor and also think about running. Does it allow freedom to do so?

Barbara Zagrodnick prepares to show Ch. Goldmedal Olympic.

Years ago, after toting around all the baby paraphernalia, I found toting the dog and necessities a breeze. You need to take along dog; crate; ex pen (if you use one); extra newspaper; water pail and water; all required grooming equipment, including hair dryer and extension cord; table; chair for you; bait for dog and lunch for you and friends; and, last but not least, clean up materials, such as plastic bags, paper towels, and perhaps a bath towel and some shampoo—just in case. Don't forget your entry confirmation and directions to the show.

If you are showing in obedience, then you will want to wear pants. Many of our top obedience handlers wear pants that are color-coordinated with their dogs. The philosophy is that imperfections in the black dog will be less obvious next to your black pants.

Whether you are showing in conformation, Junior

Showmanship or obedience, you need to watch the clock and be sure you are not

The handlers' appearance is important too—they should dress comfortably and practically.

late. It is customary to pick up your conformation armband a few minutes before the start of the class. They will not wait for you and if you are on the show grounds and not in the ring, you will upset everyone. It's a little more complicated picking up your obedience armband if you show later in the class. If you have not picked up your armband and they get to your number, you may not be allowed to show. It's best to pick up your armband early, but then you may show earlier than expected if other handlers don't pick up. Customarily all conflicts should be discussed with the judge prior to the start of the class.

The Min Pin's regal attitude makes him a striking presence in and out of the show ring.

Junior Showmanship

The Junior Showmanship Class is a wonderful way to build self confidence even if there are no aspirations of staying with the dog-show game later in life. Frequently, Junior Showmanship becomes the background of those who become successful exhibitors/handlers in the future. In some instances it is taken very seriously, and success is measured in terms of wins. The Junior Handler is judged solely on his ability and skill in presenting his dog. The dog's conformation is not to be considered by the judge. Even so the condition and grooming of the dog may be a reflection upon the handler.

Usually the matches and point shows include different classes. The Junior Handler's dog may be entered in a breed or obedience class and even shown by another person in that class. Junior Showmanship classes are usually divided by age and perhaps sex. The age is determined by the handler's age on the day of the show. The classes are:

Novice Junior for those at least ten and under 14 years of age who at time of entry closing have not won three first places in a Novice Class at a licensed or member show.

Novice Senior for those at least 14 and under 18 years of age who at the time of entry closing have not won three first places in a Novice Class at a licensed or member show.

Open Junior for those at least ten and under 14 years of age who at the time of entry closing have won at least three first places in a Novice Junior Showmanship Class at a licensed or member show with competition present.

You can begin showing your Min Pin pup as early as six months of age. In the U.S. there are two puppy classes at most shows: six to nine months and nine to twelve months.

Open Senior for those at least 14 and under 18 years of age who at time of entry closing have won at least three first places in a Novice Junior Showmanship Class at a licensed or member show with competition present.

Junior Handlers must include their AKC Junior Handler number on each show entry. This needs to be obtained from the AKC.

CERTIFICATION PROGRAMS

Two national non-competitive certification programs test a dog's behavior in simulated everyday situations. While similar in structure, the two tests are quite different. The Temperament Test (TT) evaluates untrained responses to various stimuli, while the Canine Good Citizen Test (CGC) evaluates learned behavior.

Earning the TT

A sound mind in a sound body is the motto of the American Temperament Test Society, Inc. (ATTS). Dogs that pass their ten-part test earn a certificate, and their owners proudly display the letters TT (Temperament Tested) behind the dog's name.

To pass the Temperament Test, you will take your Min Pin on a casual walk and encounter situations along the way. Neutral, friendly and threatening stimuli will test your Min Pin's ability to distinguish between nice people and harmless situations and those calling for alert and watchful reactions. If your Min Pin is well socalized, he will not need any special training for the ATTS test. For additional information, write or call: American Temperament Test Society, Inc., P.O. Box 397, Fenton, Missouri 63026, (314) 225-5346.

CANINE GOOD CITIZEN

The AKC sponsors a program to encourage dog owners to train their dogs. Local clubs perform the pass/fail tests, and dogs who pass are awarded a Canine Good Citizen Certificate. Proof of vaccination is required at the time of participation. The test includes:

1. Accepting a friendly stranger.
2. Sitting politely for petting.
3. Appearance and grooming.
4. Walking on a loose leash.
5. Walking through a crowd.
6. Sit and down on command/staying in place.

Staying down on command is part of the test for the Canine Good Citizen. This is Wil-B's Unique Lady, owned by Jean Mittardy.

7. Come when called.
8. Reaction to another dog.
9. Reactions to distractions.
10. Supervised separation.

If more effort was made by pet owners to accomplish these exercises, fewer dogs would be cast off to the humane shelter.

OBEDIENCE

Obedience is necessary, without a doubt, but it can also become a wonderful hobby or even an obsession. In my opinion, obedience classes and competition can provide wonderful companionship, not only with your dog but with your classmates or fellow competitors. It is always gratifying to discuss your dog's problems with others who have had similar experiences. The AKC acknowledged Obedience around 1936, and it has changed tremendously even though many of the exercises are basically the same. Today, obedience competition is just that—very competitive. Even so, it is possible for every obedience exhibitor to come home a winner (by earning qualifying scores) even though he/she may not earn a placement in the class.

This Min Pin earned the title Companion Dog (CD) from the Novice class, the first level in obedience competition. She is Ch. Hi-Spirit Ty Rhe,CD, owned by Velda Pearson.

Most of the obedience titles are awarded after earning three qualifying scores (legs) in the appropriate class under three different judges. These classes offer a perfect score of 200, which is extremely rare. Each of the class exercises has its own point value. A leg is earned after receiving a score of at least 170 and at least 50 percent of the points available in each exercise. The titles are:

Companion Dog—CD

This is called the Novice Class and the exercises are:

1.	Heel on leash and figure 8	40 points
2.	Stand for examination	30 points
3.	Heel free	40 points
4.	Recall	30 points
5.	Long sit—one minute	30 points
6.	Long down—three minutes	30 points
	Maximum total score	200 points

Companion Dog Excellent–CDX
This is the Open Class and the exercises are:

1.	Heel off leash and figure 8	40 points
2.	Drop on recall	30 points
3.	Retrieve on flat	20 points
4.	Retrieve over high jump	30 points
5.	Broad jump	20 points
6.	Long sit–three minutes (out of sight)	30 points
7.	Long down–five minutes (out of sight)	30 points
	Maximum total score	200 points

Utility Dog–UD
The Utility Class exercises are:

1.	Signal Exercise	40 points
2.	Scent discrimination–Article 1	30 points
3.	Scent discrimination–Article 2	30 points
4.	Directed retrieve	30 points
5.	Moving stand and examination	30 points
6.	Directed jumping	40 points
	Maximum total score	200 points

After achieving the UD title, you may feel inclined to go after the UDX and/or OTCh. The UDX (Utility Dog Excellent) title went into effect in January 1994. It is not easily attained. The title requires qualifying simultaneously ten times in Open B and Utility B but not necessarily at consecutive shows.

The OTCh (Obedience Trial Champion) is awarded after the dog has earned his UD and then goes on to earn 100 championship points, a first place in Utility, a first place in Open and another first place in either class. The placements must be won under three different judges at all-breed obedience trials. The points are determined by the number of dogs competing in the Open B and Utility B classes. The OTCh title precedes the dog's name.

Obedience matches (AKC Sanctioned, Fun, and Show and Go) are usually available. Usually they are sponsored by the local obedience clubs. When preparing an obedience dog for a title, you will find matches very helpful. Fun Matches and Show and Go Matches are more lenient in allowing you to make corrections in the ring. I frequently train (correct) in the ring and inform the judge that I would like to do so and to please mark me "exhibition." This means that I will not be eligible for any prize. This type of training is usually very necessary for the Open and Utility Classes. AKC Sanctioned Obedience Matches do not allow corrections in the ring since they must abide by the AKC Obedience Regulations. If you are interested in showing in obedience, then you should contact the AKC for a copy of the Obedience Regulations.

TRACKING

Gretchen Hofhein's Der Stutz Zelda Zing, CDX, sails over the high jump while retrieving the dumbell.

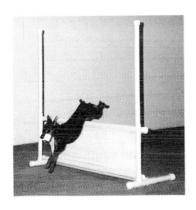

Tracking is officially classified obedience, but I feel it should have its own category. There are three tracking titles available: Tracking Dog (TD), Tracking Dog Excellent (TDX), Variable Surface Tracking (VST). If all three tracking titles are obtained, then the dog officially becomes a CT (Champion Tracker). The CT will go in front of the dog's name.

A TD may be earned anytime and does not have to follow the other obedience titles. There are many exhibitors that prefer tracking to obedience, and there are others like myself that do both. In my experience with small dogs, I prefer to earn the CD and CDX before attempting tracking. My reasoning is that small dogs are closer to the mat in the obedience rings and therefore it's too easy to put the nose down and sniff. Tracking encourages sniffing. Of course this depends on the dog. I've had some dogs that tracked around the ring and others (TDXs) who wouldn't think of sniffing in the ring.

AGILITY

Agility was first introduced by John Varley in England at the Crufts Dog Show, February 1978, but Peter Meanwell, competitor and judge, actually developed the idea. It was officially recognized in the early '80s. Agility is extremely popular in England and Canada and growing in popularity in the U.S. The AKC acknowledged agility in August 1994. Dogs must be at least 12 months of age to be entered. It is a fascinating sport that the dog, handler and spectators enjoy to the utmost. Agility is a spectator sport! The dog performs off lead. The handler either runs with his dog or positions himself on the course and directs his dog with verbal and hand signals over a timed course over or through a variety of obstacles including a time out or pause. One of the main drawbacks to agility is finding a place to train. The obstacles take up a lot of space and it is very time consuming to put up and take down courses.

The titles earned at AKC agility trials are Novice Agility Dog (NAD), Open Agility Dog (OAD), Agility Dog Excellent (ADX), and Master Agility Excellent (MAX). In order to acquire an agility title, a dog must earn a qualifying score in its respective class on three separate occasions under two different judges. The MAX will be awarded after earning ten qualifying scores in the Agility Excellent Class.

PERFORMANCE TESTS

During the last decade the American Kennel Club has promoted performance tests—those events that test the different breeds' natural abilities. This type of event encourages a handler to devote even more time to his dog and retain the natural instincts of his breed heritage. It is an important part of the wonderful world of dogs.

Performing off-lead through a variety of obstacles makes agility competition exciting not only for the dog and his handler, but for spectators as well.

GENERAL
INFORMATION
Obedience,
tracking and agility
allow the purebred
dog with an
Indefinite Listing
Privilege (ILP)
number or a limited
registration to be
exhibited and earn
titles. Application
must be made to the
AKC for an ILP
number.

Whether you enter your Min Pin in showing, obedience, tracking, or agility (as shown), he can only benefit from your attention and training.

The American Kennel Club publishes a monthly *Events* magazine that is part of the *Gazette*, their official journal for the sport of purebred dogs. The *Events* section lists upcoming shows and the secretary or superintendent for them. The majority of the conformation shows in the U.S. are overseen by licensed superintendents. Generally the entry closing date is approximately two-and-a-half weeks before the actual show. Point shows are fairly expensive, while the match shows cost about one third of the point show entry fee. Match shows usually take entries the day of the show but some are pre-entry. The best way to find match show information is through your local kennel club. Upon asking, the AKC can provide you with a list of superintendents, and you can write and ask to be put on their mailing lists.

Obedience trial and tracking test information is available through the AKC. Frequently these events are not superintended, but put on by the host club. Therefore you would make the entry with the event's secretary.

As you have read, there are numerous activities you can share with your dog. Regardless what you do, it does take teamwork. Your dog can only benefit from your attention and training. I hope this chapter has enlightened you and hope, if nothing else, you will attend a show here and there. Perhaps you will start with a puppy kindergarten class, and who knows where it may lead!

TRAVELING with Your Dog

The earlier you start traveling with your new puppy or dog, the better. He needs to become accustomed to traveling. However, some dogs are nervous riders and become carsick easily. It is helpful if he starts with an empty stomach. Do not despair, as it will go better if you continue taking him with you on short fun rides. How would you feel if every time you rode in the car you stopped at the doctor's for an injection? You would soon dread that nasty car. Older dogs that tend to get carsick may have more of a problem adjusting to traveling. Those dogs that are having a serious problem may benefit from some medication prescribed by the veterinarian.

Miles and Betty Cottle "travel" with their Min Pins in the Space Coast Therapy Dogs Parade.

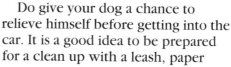

Do give your dog a chance to relieve himself before getting into the car. It is a good idea to be prepared for a clean up with a leash, paper towels, bag and terry cloth towel.

The safest place for your dog is in a fiberglass crate, although close confinement can promote carsickness in some dogs. If your dog is nervous you can try letting him ride on the seat next to you or in someone's lap.

An alternative to the crate would be to use a car harness made for dogs and/or a safety strap attached to the harness or collar. Whatever you do, do not let your dog ride in the back of a pickup truck unless he is securely tied on a very short lead. I've seen trucks stop quickly and, even though the dog was tied, it fell out and was dragged.

I do occasionally let my dogs ride loose with me because I really enjoy their companionship, but in all honesty they are safer in their crates. I have a friend whose van rolled in an

There are many safe means of traveling with your Min Pin; however, carrying him in a basket is not one of them.

accident but his dogs, in their fiberglass crates, were not injured nor did they escape. Another advantage of the crate is that it is a safe place to leave him if you need to run into the store. Otherwise you wouldn't be able to leave the windows down. Keep in mind that while many dogs are overly protective in their crates, this may not be enough to deter dognappers. In some states it is against the law to leave a dog in the car unattended.

Never leave a dog loose in the car wearing a collar and leash. I have known more than one dog that has killed himself by hanging. Do not let him put his head out an open window.

Foreign debris can be blown into his eyes. When leaving your dog unattended in a car, consider the temperature. It can take less than five minutes to reach temperatures over 100 degrees Fahrenheit.

TRIPS

Perhaps you are taking a trip. Give consideration to what is best for your dog—traveling with you or boarding. When traveling by car, van or motor home, you need to think ahead about locking your vehicle. In all probability you have many valuables in the car and do not wish to leave it unlocked. Perhaps most valuable and not replaceable is your dog. Give thought to securing your vehicle and providing adequate ventilation for him. Another consideration for you when traveling with your dog is medical problems that may arise and little inconveniences, such as exposure to external parasites. Some areas of the country are quite flea infested. You may want to carry flea spray with you. This is even a good idea when staying in motels. Quite possibly you are not the only occupant of the room.

When making arrangements to travel with your dog, call in advance to confirm that your hotel or places at your destination, like parks or tourist sites, welcome pets.

Unbelievably many motels and even hotels do allow canine guests, even some very first-class ones. Gaines Pet Foods Corporation publishes *Touring With Towser*, a directory of domestic hotels and motels that accommodate guests with dogs. Their address is Gaines TWT, PO Box 5700, Kankakee, IL, 60902. I would recommend you call ahead to any motel that you may be considering and see if they accept pets. Sometimes it is necessary to pay a deposit against room damage. Of course you are more likely to gain accommodations for a small dog than a large dog. Also the management feels reassured when you mention that your dog will be crated. Since my dogs tend to bark when I leave the room, I leave the TV on nearly full blast to deaden the noises outside that tend to encourage my dogs to bark. If you do travel with your dog, take along plenty of baggies so that you can clean up after him. When we all do our share in cleaning up, we make it possible for motels to continue accepting our

pets. As a matter of fact, you should practice cleaning up everywhere you take your dog.

Depending on where your are traveling, you may need an up-to-date health certificate issued by your veterinarian. It is good policy to take along your dog's medical information, which would include the name, address and phone number of your veterinarian, vaccination record, rabies certificate, and any medication he is taking.

AIR TRAVEL

When traveling by air, you need to contact the airlines to check their policy. Usually you have to make arrangements up to a couple of weeks in advance for traveling with your dog. The airlines require your dog to travel in an airline approved fiberglass crate. Usually these can be purchased through the airlines but they are also readily available in most pet-supply stores. If your dog is not accustomed to a crate, then it is a good idea to get him acclimated to it before your trip. The day of the actual trip you should withhold water about one hour ahead of departure and no food for about 12 hours. The airlines generally have temperature restrictions, which do not allow pets to travel if it is either too cold or too hot. Frequently these restrictions are based on the temperatures at the departure and arrival airports. It's best to inquire about a health certificate. These usually need to be issued within ten days of departure. You should arrange for non-stop, direct flights and if a commuter plane should be involved, check to see if it will carry dogs. Some don't. The Humane Society of the United States has put together a tip sheet for airline traveling. You can receive a copy by sending a self-addressed stamped envelope to:

The Humane Society of the United States
Tip Sheet
2100 L Street NW
Washington, DC 20037.

No matter how much your Min Pin begs, don't feed him within twelve hours of traveling by air. Water should be withheld one hour prior to departure.

In preparation for a trip, your Min Pin should be in top health, he should be clean and flea-free, and his vaccinations should be up to date.

Regulations differ for traveling outside of the country and are sometimes changed without notice. Well in advance you need to write or call the appropriate consulate or agricultural department for instructions. Some countries have lengthy quarantines (six months), and countries differ in their rabies vaccination requirements. For instance, it may have to be given at least 30 days ahead of your departure.

Do make sure your dog is wearing proper identification. You never know when you might be in an accident and separated from your dog. Or your dog could be frightened and somehow manage to escape and run away. When I travel, my dogs wear collars with engraved nameplates with my name, phone number and city.

Another suggestion would be to carry in-case-of-emergency instructions. These would include the address and phone number of a relative or friend, your veterinarian's name, address and phone number, and your dog's medical information.

BOARDING KENNELS

Perhaps you have decided that you need to board your dog. Your veterinarian can recommend a good boarding facility or possibly a pet sitter that will come to your house. It is customary for the boarding kennel to ask for proof of vaccination for the DHLPP, rabies and bordetella vaccine. The bordetella should have been given within six months of boarding. This is for your protection. If they do not ask for this proof I would not board at their kennel. Ask about flea control. Those dogs that suffer flea-bite allergy can get in trouble at a boarding kennel. Unfortunately boarding kennels are limited on how much they are able to do.

If you are traveling and must leave your dog behind, there are two options for care: a kennel or a qualified pet sitter.

For more information on pet sitting, contact NAPPS:
National Association of Professional Pet Sitters
1200 G Street, NW
Suite 760
Washington, DC 20005.

Our clinic has technicians that pet sit and technicians that board clinic patients in their homes. This may be an alternative for you. Ask your veterinarian if they have an employee that can help you. There is a definite advantage of having a technician care for your dog, especially if your dog is on medication or is a senior citizen.

You can write for a copy of *Traveling With Your Pet* from ASPCA, Education Department, 441 E. 92nd Street, New York, NY 10128.

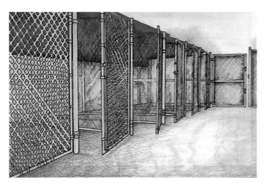

A reputable boarding kennel will require that dogs receive the vaccination for kennel cough no less than two weeks before their scheduled stay.

IDENTIFICATION and Finding the Lost Dog

There are several ways of identifying your dog. The old standby is a collar with dog license, rabies, and ID tags. Unfortunately collars have a way of being separated from the dog and tags fall off. I am not suggesting you shouldn't use a collar and tags. If they stay intact and on the dog, they are the quickest way of identification.

For several years owners have been tattooing their dogs. Some tattoos use a number with a registry. Here lies the problem because there are several registries to check. If you wish to tattoo, use your social security number. The humane shelters have the means to trace it. It is usually done on the inside of the rear thigh. The area is first shaved and numbed. There is no pain, although a few dogs do not like the buzzing sound. Occasionally tattooing is not legible and needs to be redone.

The newest method of identification is microchipping. The microchip is a computer chip that is no larger than a grain of rice. The veterinarian implants it by injection between the shoulder blades. The dog feels no discomfort. If your dog is lost and picked up by the humane society, they can trace you by scanning the microchip, which has its own code. Microchip scanners are friendly to other brands of microchips and their registries. The microchip comes with a dog tag saying the dog is microchipped. It is the safest way of identifying your dog.

FINDING THE LOST DOG

I am sure you will agree with me that there would be little worse than losing your dog. Responsible pet owners rarely lose their dogs. They do not let their dogs run free because they don't want harm to come to them. Not only that but in most, if not all, states there is a leash law.

Beware of fenced-in yards. They can be a hazard. Dogs find ways to escape either over or under the fence. Another fast exit is through the gate that perhaps the neighbor's child left unlocked.

Below is a list that hopefully will be of help to you if you need it. Remember don't give up, keep looking. Your dog is worth your efforts.

Make sure your Min Pin has a collar with the proper tags, or some means of identification, in case he gets lost.

1. Contact your neighbors and put flyers with a photo on it in their mailboxes. Information you should include would be the dog's name, breed, sex, color, age, source of identification, when your dog was last seen and where, and your name and phone numbers. It may be helpful to say the dog needs medical care. Offer a *reward*.

2. Check all local shelters daily. It is also possible for your dog to be picked up away from home and end up in an out-of-the-way shelter. Check these too. Go in person. It is not good enough to call. Most shelters are limited on the time they can hold dogs then they are put up for adoption or euthanized. There is the possibility that your dog will not make it to the shelter for several days. Your dog could have been wandering or someone may have tried to keep him.

3. Notify all local veterinarians. Call and send flyers.

4. Call your breeder. Frequently breeders are contacted when one of their breed is found.

5. Contact the rescue group for your breed.

6. Contact local schools—children may have seen your dog.

7. Post flyers at the schools, groceries, gas stations, convenience stores, veterinary clinics, groomers and any other place that will allow them.

8. Advertise in the newspaper.

9. Advertise on the radio.

DENTAL CARE for Your Dog's Life

So you've got a new puppy! You also have a new set of puppy teeth in your household. Anyone who has ever raised a puppy is abundantly aware of these new teeth. Your puppy will chew anything it can reach, chase your shoelaces, and play "tear the rag" with any piece of clothing it can find. When puppies are newly born, they have no teeth. At about four weeks of age, puppies of most breeds begin to develop their deciduous or baby teeth. They begin eating semi-solid food, fighting and biting with their litter mates, and learning discipline from their mother. As their new teeth come in, they inflict more pain on their mother's breasts, so her feeding sessions become less frequent and shorter. By six or eight weeks, the mother will start growling to warn her pups when they are fighting too roughly or hurting her as they nurse too much with their new teeth.

Maintaining healthy teeth and gums is an important part of your dog's general care. Check and brush his teeth regularly.

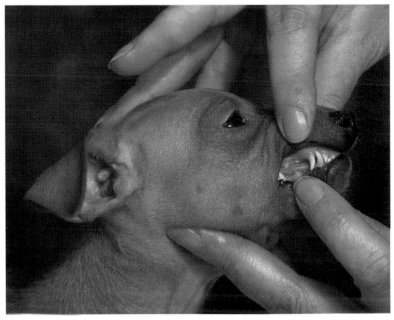

Chewing for puppies is a natural part of their development. Just make sure there are enough chewable toys around so your Min Pin won't go after your sweaters.

Puppies need to chew. It is a necessary part of their physical and mental development. They develop muscles and necessary life skills as they drag objects around, fight over possession, and vocalize alerts and warnings. Puppies chew on things to explore their world. They are using their sense of taste to determine what is food and what is not. How else can they tell an electrical cord from a lizard? At about four months of age, most puppies begin shedding their baby teeth. Often these teeth need some help to come out and make way for the permanent teeth. The incisors (front teeth) will be replaced first. Then, the adult canine or fang teeth erupt. When the baby tooth is not shed before the permanent tooth comes in, veterinarians call it a retained deciduous tooth. This condition will often cause gum infections by trapping hair and debris between the permanent tooth and the retained baby tooth. Nylafloss® is an excellent device for puppies to use. They can toss it, drag it, and chew on the many surfaces it presents. The baby teeth can catch in the nylon material, aiding in their removal. Puppies that have adequate chew toys will have less destructive behavior, develop more physically, and have less chance of retained deciduous teeth.

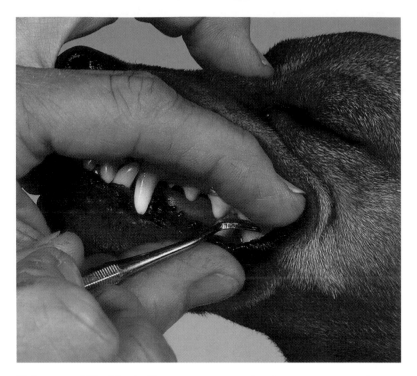

Take your Min Pin to the veterinarian for regular dental checkups so he can check for sores, tooth problems, and general oral health.

During the first year, your dog should be seen by your veterinarian at regular intervals. Your veterinarian will let you know when to bring in your puppy for vaccinations and parasite examinations. At each visit, your veterinarian should inspect the lips, teeth, and mouth as part of a complete physical examination. You should take some part in the maintenance of your dog's oral health. You should examine your dog's mouth weekly throughout his first year to make sure there are no sores, foreign objects, tooth problems, etc. If your dog drools excessively, shakes its head, or has bad breath, consult your veterinarian. By the time your dog is six months old, the permanent teeth are all in and plaque can start to accumulate on the tooth surfaces. This is when your dog needs to develop good dental-care habits to prevent calculus build-up on his teeth. Brushing is best. That is a fact that cannot be denied.

However, some dogs do not like their teeth brushed regularly, or you may not be able to accomplish the task. In that case, you should consider a product that will help prevent plaque and calculus build-up.

The Plaque Attackers® and Galileo Bone® are other excellent choices for the first three years of a dog's life. Their shapes make them interesting for the dog. As the dog chews on them, the solid polyurethane massages the gums which improves the blood circulation to the periodontal tissues. Projections on the chew devices increase the surface and are in contact with the tooth for more efficient cleaning. The unique shape and consistency prevent your dog from exerting excessive force on his own teeth or from breaking off pieces of the bone. If your dog is an aggressive chewer or weighs more than 55 pounds (25 kg), you should consider giving him a Nylabone®, the most durable chew product on the market.

The Gumabone ®, made by the Nylabone Company, is constructed of strong polyurethane, which is softer than nylon. Less powerful chewers prefer the Gumabones® to the Nylabones®. A super option for your dog is the Hercules Bone®, a uniquely shaped bone named after the great Olympian for its

Safe chew toys not only keep your Min Pin's teeth clean, but also relieve stress and provide your dog with entertainment.

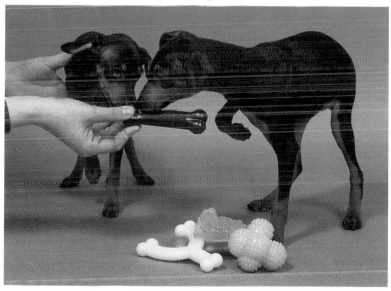

exceptional strength. Like all Nylabone products, they are specially scented to make them attractive to your dog. Ask your veterinarian about these bones and he will validate the good doctor's prescription: Nylabones® not only give your dog a good chewing workout but also help to save your dog's teeth (and even his life, as it protects him from possible fatal periodontal diseases).

By the time dogs are four years old, 75% of them have periodontal disease. It is the most common infection in dogs. Yearly examinations by your veterinarian are essential to maintaining your dog's good health. If your veterinarian detects periodontal disease, he or she may recommend a prophylactic cleaning. To do a thorough cleaning, it will be necessary to put your dog under anesthesia. With modern gas anesthetics and monitoring equipment, the procedure is pretty safe. Your veterinarian will scale the teeth with an ultrasound scaler or hand instrument. This removes the calculus from the teeth. If there are calculus deposits below the gum line, the veterinarian will plane the roots to make them smooth. After all of the calculus has been removed, the teeth are polished with pumice in a polishing cup. If any medical or surgical

As your dog ages, his teeth and gums should be professionally examined and cleaned frequently.

treatment is needed, it is done at this time. The final step would be fluoride treatment and your follow-up treatment at home. If the periodontal disease is advanced, the veterinarian may prescribe a medicated mouth rinse or antibiotics for use at home. Make sure your dog has safe, clean and attractive chew toys and treats. Chooz® treats are another way of using a consumable treat to help keep your dog's teeth clean.

As your dog ages, professional examination and cleaning should become more frequent. The mouth should be inspected at least once a year. Your veterinarian may recommend visits every six months. In the geriatric patient, organs such as the heart, liver, and kidneys do not function as well as when they were young. Your veterinarian will probably want to test these organs' functions prior to using general anesthesia for dental cleaning. If your dog is a good chewer and you work closely with your veterinarian, your dog can keep all of its teeth all of its life. However, as your dog ages, his sense of smell, sight, and taste will diminish. He may not have the desire to chase, trap or chew his toys. He will also not have the energy to chew for long periods, as arthritis and periodontal disease make chewing painful. This will leave you with more responsibility for keeping his teeth clean and healthy. The dog that would not let you brush his teeth at one year of age, may let you brush his teeth now that he is ten years old.

Teach your Min Pin constructive chewing habits by providing him with an array of Nylabone® products like a colorful Gumabone®.

If you train your dog with good chewing habits as a puppy, he will have healthier teeth throughout his life.

HEALTH CARE

Veterinary medicine has become far more sophisticated than what was available to our ancestors. This can be attributed to the increase in household pets and consequently the demand for better care for them. Also human medicine has become far more complex. Today diagnostic testing in veterinary medicine parallels human diagnostics. Because of better technology we can expect our pets to live healthier lives thereby increasing their life spans.

THE FIRST CHECK UP

You will want to take your new puppy/dog in for its first check up within 48 to 72 hours after acquiring it. Many breeders strongly recommend this check up and so do the humane shelters. A puppy/dog can appear healthy but it may

You should bring your new pet to a veterinarian for his first check up within two to three days of bringing him home.

have a serious problem that is not apparent to the layman. Most pets have some type of a minor flaw that may never cause a real problem.

Unfortunately if he/she should have a serious problem, you will want to consider the consequences of keeping the pet and the attachments that will be formed, which may be broken prematurely. Keep in mind there are many healthy dogs looking for good homes.

Your pet will be given a thorough examination of his eyes, ears, teeth, heart, skin and coat.

This first check up is a good time to establish yourself with the veterinarian and learn the office policy regarding their hours and how they handle emergencies. Usually the breeder or another conscientious pet owner is a good reference for locating a capable veterinarian. You should be aware that not all veterinarians give the same quality of service. Please do not make your selection on the least expensive clinic, as they may be short changing your pet. There is the possibility that eventually it will cost you more due to improper diagnosis, treatment, etc. If you are selecting a new veterinarian, feel free to ask for a tour of the clinic. You should inquire about making an appointment for a tour since all clinics are working clinics, and therefore may not be available all day for sightseers. You may worry less if you see where your pet will be spending the day if he ever needs to be hospitalized.

THE PHYSICAL EXAM

Your veterinarian will check your pet's overall condition, which includes listening to the heart; checking the respiration; feeling the abdomen, muscles and joints; checking the mouth, which includes the gum color and signs of gum disease along with plaque buildup; checking the ears for signs of an infection or ear mites; examining the eyes; and, last but not least, checking the condition of the skin and coat.

He should ask you questions regarding your pet's eating and elimination habits and invite you to relay your questions. It is a good idea to prepare a list so as not to forget anything. He should discuss the proper diet and the quantity to be fed. If this should differ from your breeder's recommendation, then you should convey to him the breeder's choice and see if he approves. If he recommends changing the diet, then this should be done over a few days so as not to cause a gastrointestinal upset. It is customary to take in a fresh stool sample (just a small amount) for a test for intestinal parasites. It must be fresh, preferably within 12 hours, since the eggs hatch quickly and after hatching will not be observed under the microscope. If your pet isn't obliging then, usually the technician can take one in the clinic.

IMMUNIZATIONS

It is important that you take your puppy/dog's vaccination record with you on your first visit. In case of a puppy, presumably the breeder has seen to the vaccinations up to the time you acquired custody. Veterinarians differ in their vaccination protocol. It is not unusual for your puppy to have received vaccinations for distemper, hepatitis, leptospirosis, parvovirus and parainfluenza every two to three weeks from the age of five or six weeks. Usually this is a combined injection and is typically called the DHLPP. The DHLPP is given through at least 12 to 14 weeks of age, and it is customary to continue with another parvovirus vaccine at 16 to 18 weeks. You may wonder why so many immunizations are necessary. No one knows for sure when the puppy's maternal antibodies are gone, although it is customarily accepted that distemper antibodies are gone by 12 weeks. Usually parvovirus antibodies are gone by 16 to 18 weeks of age. However, it is possible for the maternal antibodies to be gone at a much earlier age or even a later age. Therefore immunizations are started at an early

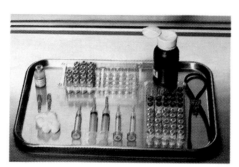

It is extremely important that your Min Pin is properly vaccinated. Take him to the veterinarian to get him started on a vaccination schedule.

Puppies receive maternal antibodies for certain diseases, but they are usually gone by 12 weeks of age. Immunizations are begun early to provide immunity when these run out.

age. The vaccine will not give immunity as long as there are maternal antibodies.

The rabies vaccination is given at three or six months of age depending on your local laws. A vaccine for bordetella (kennel cough) is advisable and can be given anytime from the age of five weeks. The coronavirus is not commonly given unless there is a problem locally. The Lyme vaccine is necessary in endemic areas. Lyme disease has been reported in 47 states.

Distemper

This is virtually an incurable disease. If the dog recovers, he is subject to severe nervous disorders. The virus attacks every tissue in the body and resembles a bad cold with a fever. It can cause a runny nose and eyes and cause gastrointestinal disorders, including a poor appetite, vomiting and diarrhea. The virus is carried by raccoons, foxes, wolves, mink and other dogs. Unvaccinated youngsters and senior citizens are very susceptible. This is still a common disease.

Hepatitis

This is a virus that is most serious in very young dogs. It is spread by contact with an infected animal or its stool or urine. The virus affects the liver and kidneys and is characterized by high fever, depression and lack of appetite. Recovered animals may be afflicted with chronic illnesses.

Leptospirosis

This is a bacterial disease transmitted by contact with the urine of an infected dog, rat or other wildlife. It produces severe symptoms of fever, depression, jaundice and internal bleeding and was fatal before the vaccine was developed. Recovered dogs can be carriers, and the disease can be transmitted from dogs to humans.

Laboratory tests are studied by highly trained veterinary technicians. Most tests are performed right in the vet's office, and results are usually made available the same day.

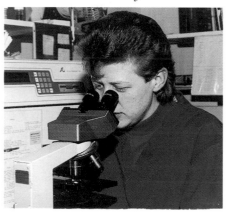

Parvovirus

This was first noted in the late 1970s and is still a fatal disease. However, with proper vaccinations, early diagnosis and prompt treatment, it is a manageable disease. It attacks the bone marrow and intestinal tract. The symptoms include depression, loss of appetite, vomiting, diarrhea and collapse. Immediate medical attention is of the essence.

Rabies

This is shed in the saliva and is carried by raccoons, skunks, foxes, other dogs and cats. It attacks nerve tissue, resulting in paralysis and death. Rabies can be transmitted to people and is virtually always fatal. This disease is reappearing in the suburbs.

Many viral infections can be acquired when dogs are kept in close quarters. Make sure that your Min Pin is healthy and properly vaccinated.

Bordetella (Kennel Cough)

The symptoms are coughing, sneezing, hacking and retching accompanied by nasal discharge usually lasting from a few days to several weeks. There are several disease-producing organisms responsible for this disease. The present vaccines are helpful but do not protect for all the strains. It usually is not life threatening but in some instances it can progress to a serious bronchopneumonia. The disease is highly contagious. The vaccination should be given routinely for dogs that come in contact with other dogs, such as through boarding, training class or visits to the groomer.

Coronavirus

This is usually self limiting and not life threatening. It was first noted in the late '70s about a year before parvovirus.

The virus produces a yellow/brown stool and there may be depression, vomiting and diarrhea.

Lyme Disease

This was first diagnosed in the United States in 1976 in Lyme, CT in people who lived in close proximity to the deer tick. Symptoms may include acute lameness, fever, swelling of joints and loss of appetite. Your veterinarian can advise you if you live in an endemic area.

After your puppy has completed his puppy vaccinations, you will continue to booster the DHLPP once a year. It is customary to booster the rabies one year after the first vaccine and then, depending on where you live, it should be boostered every year or every three years. This depends on your local laws. The Lyme and corona vaccines are boostered annually and it is recommended that the bordetella be boostered every six to eight months.

ANNUAL VISIT

I would like to impress the importance of the annual check up, which would include the booster vaccinations, check for intestinal parasites and test for heartworm. Today in our very busy world it is rush, rush and see "how much you can get for how little." Unbelievably, some non-veterinary businesses have entered into the vaccination business. More harm than good can come to your dog through improper vaccinations, possibly from inferior vaccines and/or the wrong schedule. More than likely you truly care about your companion dog and over the years you have devoted much time and expense to his well being. Perhaps you are unaware that a vaccination is not just a vaccination. There is more involved. Please, please follow through with regular physical examinations. It is so important for your veterinarian to know your dog and this is especially true during middle age through the geriatric years. More than likely your older dog will require more than one physical a year. The annual physical is good preventive medicine. Through early diagnosis and subsequent treatment your dog can maintain a longer and better quality of life.

Hookworms

These are almost microscopic intestinal worms that can cause anemia and therefore serious problems, including death, in young puppies. Hookworms can be transmitted to humans through penetration of the skin. Puppies may be born with them.

Roundworms

These are spaghetti-like worms that can cause a potbellied appearance and dull coat along with more severe symptoms, such as vomiting, diarrhea and coughing. Puppies acquire these while in the mother's uterus and through lactation. Both hookworms and roundworms may be acquired through ingestion.

If your Min Pin spends time outdoors, make sure to use some form of protection against fleas, and check his skin and coat for ticks before he comes in.

Whipworms

These have a three-month life cycle and are not acquired through the dam. They cause intermittent

diarrhea usually with mucus. Whipworms are possibly the most difficult worm to eradicate. Their eggs are very resistant to most environmental factors and can last for years until the proper conditions enable them to mature. Whipworms are seldom seen in the stool.

Intestinal parasites are more prevalent in some areas than others. Climate, soil and contamination are big factors contributing to the incidence of intestinal parasites. Eggs are passed in the stool, lay on the ground and then become infective in a certain number of days. Each of the above worms has a different life cycle. Your best chance of becoming and remaining worm-free is to always pooper-scoop your yard. A fenced-in yard keeps stray dogs out, which is certainly helpful.

You will often be able to recognize if your dog is sick by a drop in activity level or a loss of appetite—something these dogs don't suffer from!

I would recommend having a fecal examination on your dog twice a year or more often if there is a problem. If your dog has a positive fecal sample, then he will be given the appropriate medication and you will be asked to bring back another stool sample in a certain period of time (depending on the type of worm) and then be rewormed. This process goes on until he has at least two negative samples. The different types of worms require different medications. You will be wasting your money and doing your dog an injustice by buying over-the-counter medication without first consulting your veterinarian.

OTHER INTERNAL PARASITES

Coccidiosis and Giardiasis

These protozoal infections usually affect puppies, especially in places where large numbers of puppies are brought together. Older dogs may harbor these infections but do not show signs unless they are stressed. Symptoms include diarrhea, weight loss and lack of appetite. These infections are not always apparent in the fecal examination.

Tapeworms

Seldom apparent on fecal floatation, they are diagnosed frequently as rice-like segments around the dog's anus and the base of the tail. Tapeworms are long, flat and ribbon-like, sometimes several feet in length, and made up of many segments about five-eighths of an inch long. The two most common types of tapeworms found in the dog are:

(1) First the larval form of the flea tapeworm parasite must mature in an intermediate host, the flea, before it can become infective. Your dog acquires this by ingesting the flea through licking and chewing.

(2) Rabbits, rodents and certain large game animals serve as intermediate hosts for other species of tapeworms. If your dog should eat one of these infected hosts, then he can acquire tapeworms.

HEARTWORM DISEASE

This is a worm that resides in the heart and adjacent blood vessels of the lung that produces microfilaria, which circulate

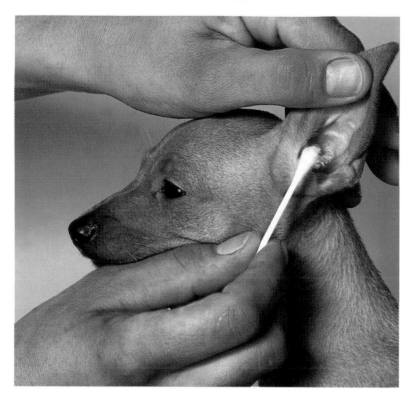

Routinely check your Min Pin's skin and coat, as well as ears, for parasites or infection.

in the bloodstream. It is possible for a dog to be infected with any number of worms from one to a hundred that can be 6 to 14 inches long. It is a life-threatening disease, expensive to treat and easily prevented. Depending on where you live, your veterinarian may recommend a preventive year-round and either an annual or semiannual blood test. The most common preventive is given once a month.

EXTERNAL PARASITES

Fleas

These pests are not only the dog's worst enemy but also enemy to the owner's pocketbook. Preventing is less expensive than treating, but regardless I think we'd prefer to spend our money elsewhere. I would guess that the majority of our dogs are allergic to the bite of a flea, and in many cases it only takes one flea bite. The protein in the flea's saliva is the culprit. Allergic dogs have a reaction, which usually results in a "hot spot." More than likely such a reaction will involve a trip to the veterinarian for treatment. Yes, prevention is less expensive. Fortunately today there are several good products available.

If there is a flea infestation, no one product is going to correct the problem. Not only will the dog require treatment so will the environment. In general flea collars are not very effective although there is now available an "egg" collar that will kill the eggs on the dog. Dips are the most economical but they are messy. There are some effective shampoos and treatments available through pet shops and veterinarians. An oral tablet arrived on the American market in 1995 and was popular in Europe the previous year. It sterilizes the female flea but will not kill adult fleas. Therefore the tablet, which is given monthly, will decrease the flea population but is not a "cure-all." Those dogs that suffer from flea-bite allergy will still be subjected to the bite of the flea. Another popular parasiticide is permethrin, which is applied to the back of the dog in one or two places depending on the dog's weight. This product works as a repellent causing the flea to get "hot feet" and jump off. Do not confuse this product with some of the organophosphates that are also applied to the dog's back.

The best approach to prevent and eliminate a flea infestation is to use a safe insecticide to kill adult fleas in the house and then an insect growth regulator to stop the eggs and larvae in the environment.

Some products are not usable on young puppies. Treating fleas should be done under your veterinarian's guidance. Frequently it is necessary to combine products and the layman does not have the knowledge regarding possible toxicities. It is hard to believe but there are a few dogs that do have a natural resistance to fleas. Nevertheless it would be wise to treat all pets at the same time. Don't forget your cats. Cats just love to prowl the neighborhood and consequently return with unwanted guests.

Adult fleas live on the dog but their eggs drop off the dog into the environment. There they go through four larval stages before reaching adulthood, and thereby are able to jump back on the poor unsuspecting dog. The cycle resumes and takes between 21 to 28 days under ideal conditions. There are environmental products available that will kill both the adult fleas and the larvae.

Ticks

Ticks carry Rocky Mountain Spotted Fever, Lyme disease and can cause tick paralysis. They should be removed with tweezers, trying to pull out the head. The jaws carry disease. There is a tick preventive collar that does an excellent job. The ticks automatically back out on those dogs wearing collars.

Sarcoptic Mange

This is a mite that is difficult to find on skin scrapings. The pinnal reflex is a good indicator of this disease. Rub the ends of the pinna (ear) together and the dog will start scratching with his foot. Sarcoptes are highly contagious to other dogs and to humans although they do not live long on humans. They cause intense itching.

Demodectic Mange

This is a mite that is passed from the dam to her puppies. It affects youngsters age three to ten months. Diagnosis is

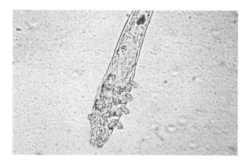

The demodex mite is passed from the dam to her puppies. It affects youngsters from the ages of three to ten months.

confirmed by skin scraping. Small areas of alopecia around the eyes, lips and/or forelegs become visible. There is little itching unless there is a secondary bacterial infection. Some breeds are afflicted more than others.

Cheyletiella

This causes intense itching and is diagnosed by skin scraping. It lives in the outer layers of the skin of dogs, cats, rabbits and humans. Yellow-gray scales may be found on the back and the rump, top of the head and the nose.

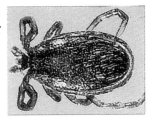

The deer tick is the most common carrier of Lyme disease. Your veterinarian can advise you if you live in an endemic area. Photo courtesy of Virbac Laboratories, Inc., Fort Worth, Texas.

TO BREED OR NOT TO BREED

More than likely your breeder has requested that you have your puppy neutered or spayed. Your breeder's request is based on what is healthiest for your dog and what is most beneficial for your breed. Experienced and conscientious breeders devote many years into developing a bloodline. In order to do this, he makes every effort to plan each breeding in regard to conformation, temperament and health. This type of breeder does his best to perform the necessary testing (i.e., OFA, CERF, testing for inherited blood disorders, thyroid, etc.). Testing is expensive and sometimes very disheartening when a favorite dog doesn't pass his health tests. The health history pertains not only to the breeding stock but to the immediate ancestors. Reputable breeders do not want their offspring to be bred indiscriminately. Therefore you may be asked to neuter or spay your puppy. Of course there is always the exception, and your breeder may agree to let you breed your dog under his direct supervision. This is an important concept. More and more effort is being made to breed healthier dogs.

Spay/Neuter

There are numerous benefits of performing this surgery at six months of age. Unspayed females are subject to mammary and ovarian cancer. In order to prevent mammary cancer she must be spayed prior to her first heat cycle. Later in life, an unspayed female may develop a pyometra (an infected uterus), which is definitely life threatening.

Spaying is performed under a general anesthetic and is easy on the young dog. As you might expect it is a little harder on the older dog, but that is no reason to deny her the surgery. The surgery removes the ovaries and uterus. It is important to remove all the ovarian tissue. If some is left behind, she could remain attractive to males. In order to view the ovaries, a reasonably long incision is necessary. An ovariohysterectomy is considered major surgery.

Neutering the male at a young age will inhibit some characteristic male behavior that owners frown upon. I have found my boys will not hike their legs and mark territory if they are neutered at six months of age. Also neutering at a young age has hormonal benefits, lessening the chance of hormonal aggressiveness.

Surgery involves removing the testicles but leaving the scrotum. If there should be a retained testicle, then he definitely needs to be neutered before the age of two or three years. Retained testicles can develop into cancer. Unneutered males are at risk for testicular cancer, perineal fistulas, perianal tumors and fistulas and prostatic disease.

Intact males and females are prone to housebreaking accidents. Females urinate frequently before, during and after heat cycles, and males tend to mark territory if there is a female in heat. Males may show the same behavior if there is a visiting dog or guests.

Surgery involves a sterile operating

Having your puppy spayed or neutered eliminates the risk of cancer of the reproductive organs later in life.

If you do decide to breed your female Min Pin, wait until at least her second or third heat cycle.

procedure equivalent to human surgery. The incision site is shaved, surgically scrubbed and draped. The veterinarian wears a sterile surgical gown, cap, mask and gloves.

Anesthesia should be monitored by a registered technician. It is customary for the veterinarian to recommend a pre-anesthetic blood screening, looking for metabolic problems and a ECG rhythm strip to check for normal heart function. Today anesthetics are equal to human anesthetics, which enables your dog to walk out of the clinic the same day as surgery.

Some folks worry about their dog gaining weight after being neutered or spayed. This is usually not the case. It is true that some dogs may be less active so they could develop a problem, but my own dogs are just as active as they were before surgery. I have a hard time keeping weight on them. However, if your dog should begin to gain, then you need to decrease his food and see to it that he gets a little more exercise.

BEHAVIOR and Canine Communication

Studies of the human/animal bond point out the importance of the unique relationships that exist between people and their pets. Those of us who share our lives with pets understand the special part they play through companionship, service and protection. For many, the pet/owner bond goes beyond simple companionship; pets are often considered members of the family. A leading pet food manufacturer recently conducted a nationwide survey of pet owners to gauge just how important pets were in their lives. Here's what they found:

- 76 percent allow their pets to sleep on their beds
- 78 percent think of their pets as their children
- 84 percent display photos of their pets mostly in their homes.
- 100 percent talk to their pets
- 97 percent think that their pets understand what they're saying

Are you surprised?

Senior citizens show more concern for their own eating habits when they have the responsibility of feeding a dog. Seeing that their dog is routinely exercised encourages the owner to think of schedules that otherwise may seem unimportant to the senior citizen. The older owner may be arthritic and feeling poorly but with responsibility for his dog he has a reason to get up and get moving. It is a big plus if his dog is an attention seeker who will demand such from his owner.

Over the last couple of decades, it has been shown that pets relieve the stress of those who lead busy lives. Owning a pet has been known to lessen the occurrence of heart attack and stroke.

Many single folks thrive on the companionship of a dog. Lifestyles are very different from a long time ago, and today more individuals seek the single life. However, they receive fulfillment from owning a dog.

Most likely the majority of our dogs live in family environments. The companionship they provide is well worth the effort involved. In my opinion, every child should have the opportunity to have a family dog. Dogs teach responsibility through understanding their care, feelings and even respecting their life cycles. Frequently those children who have not been exposed to dogs grow up afraid of dogs, which isn't good. Dogs sense timidity and some will take advantage of the situation.

Today more dogs are serving as service dogs. Since the origination of the Seeing Eye dogs years ago, we now have trained hearing dogs. Also dogs are trained to provide service for the handicapped and are able to perform many different tasks for their owners. Search and Rescue dogs, with their handlers, are sent throughout the world to assist in recovery of disaster victims. They are life savers.

Children and Min Pins make great playmates—as long as the child is taught to handle the dog with care.

Therapy dogs are very popular with nursing homes, and some hospitals even allow them to visit. The inhabitants truly look forward to their visits. I have taken a couple of my dogs visiting and left in tears when I saw the response of the patients. They wanted and were allowed to have my dogs in their beds to hold and love.

Nationally there is a Pet Awareness Week to educate students and others about the value and basic care of our pets. Many countries take an even greater interest in their pets than Americans do. In those countries the pets are allowed to accompany their owners into restaurants and shops, etc. In the U.S. this freedom is only available to our service dogs. Even so we think very highly of the human/animal bond.

CANINE BEHAVIOR

Canine behavior problems are the number-one reason for pet owners to dispose of their dogs, either through new homes, humane shelters or euthanasia. Unfortunately there are too many owners who are unwilling to devote the necessary time to properly train their dogs. On the other hand, there are those who not only are concerned about inherited health problems but are also aware of the dog's mental stability.

You may realize that a breed and his group relatives (i.e., sporting, hounds, etc.) show tendencies to behavioral characteristics. An experienced breeder can acquaint you with his breed's personality. Unfortunately many breeds are labeled with poor temperaments when actually the breed as a whole is not affected but only a small percentage of individuals within the breed.

If the breed in question is very popular, then of course there may be a higher number of unstable dogs. Do not label a breed good or bad. I know of absolutely awful-tempered dogs within one of our most popular, lovable breeds.

Inheritance and environment contribute to the dog's behavior. Some naive people suggest inbreeding as the cause of bad temperaments. Inbreeding only results in poor behavior if the ancestors carry the trait. If there are excellent temperaments behind the dogs, then inbreeding will promote good temperaments in the offspring. Did you ever consider that inbreeding is what sets the characteristics of a breed? A purebred dog is the end result of inbreeding. This does not spare the mixed-breed dog from the same problems. Mixed-breed dogs frequently are the offspring of purebred dogs.

When planning a breeding, I like to observe the potential stud and his offspring in the show ring. If I see unruly behavior, I try to look into it further. I want to know if it is genetic or environmental, due to the lack of training and

Upbringing and environment will both play a part in the adult temperament of these young pups; however, the temperament of the parents is usually passed on to their young.

146

socialization. A good breeder will avoid breeding mentally unsound dogs.

Not too many decades ago most of our dogs led a different lifestyle than what is prevalent today. Usually mom stayed home so the dog had human companionship and someone to discipline it if needed. Not much was expected from the dog. Today's mom works and everyone's life is at a much faster pace.

The dog may have to adjust to being a "weekend" dog.

Your Min Pin needs lots of exercise and love to be happy.

The family is gone all day during the week, and the dog is left to his own devices for entertainment. Some dogs sleep all day waiting for their family to

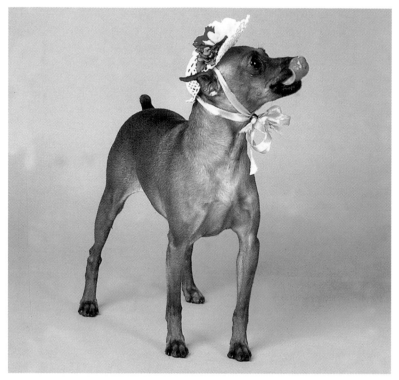

No matter how much people would like to believe otherwise, they must remember that their Min Pin is a dog, and not a person.

come home and others become wigwam wreckers if given the opportunity. Crates do ensure the safety of the dog and the house. However, he could become physically and emotionally crippled if he doesn't get enough exercise and attention. We still appreciate and want the companionship of our dogs although we expect more from them. In many cases we tend to forget dogs are just that—*dogs* not human beings.

I own several dogs who are left crated during the day but I do try to make time for them in the evenings and on the weekends. Also we try to do something together before I leave for work. Maybe it helps them to have the companionship of other dogs. They accept their crates as their personal "houses" and seem to be content with their routine and thrive on trying their best to please me.

SOCIALIZING AND TRAINING

Many prospective puppy buyers lack experience regarding the proper socialization and training needed to develop the type of pet we all desire. In the first 18 months, training does take some work. Trust me, it is easier to start proper training before there is a problem that needs to be corrected.

The initial work begins with the breeder. The breeder should start socializing the puppy at five to six weeks of age and cannot let up. Human socializing is critical up through 12 weeks of age and likewise important during the following months. The litter should be left together during the first few weeks but it is necessary to separate them by ten weeks of age. Leaving them together after that time will increase competition for litter dominance. If puppies are not socialized with people by 12 weeks of age, they will be timid in later life.

In order to properly socialize your puppy, introduce him not only to adults and children but also to other dogs, after he is properly vaccinated.

The eight- to ten-week age period is a fearful time for puppies. They need to be handled very gently around children and adults. There should be no harsh discipline during this time. Starting at 14 weeks of age, the puppy begins the juvenile period, which ends when he reaches sexual maturity around six to 14 months of age. During the juvenile period he needs to be introduced to strangers (adults, children and other dogs) on the home property. At sexual maturity he will begin to bark at strangers and become more protective. Males start to lift their legs to urinate but if you desire you can inhibit this behavior by walking your boy on leash away from trees, shrubs, fences, etc.

Perhaps you are thinking about an older puppy. You need to inquire about the puppy's social experience. If he has lived in a kennel, he may have a hard time adjusting to people and environmental stimuli. Assuming he has had a good social upbringing, there are advantages to an older puppy.

Training includes puppy kindergarten and a minimum of one to two basic training classes. During these classes you will learn how to dominate your youngster. This is especially important if you own a large breed of dog. It is somewhat harder, if not nearly impossible, for some owners to be the Alpha figure when their dog towers over them. You will be taught how to properly restrain your dog. This concept is important. Again it puts you in the Alpha position. All dogs need to be restrained many times during their lives. Believe it or not, some of our worst offenders are the eight-week-old puppies that are brought to our clinic. They need to be gently restrained for a nail trim but the way they carry on you would think we were killing them. In comparison, their vaccination is a "piece of cake." When we ask dogs to do something that is not agreeable to them, then their worst comes out.

Life will be easier for your dog if you expose him at a young age to the necessities of life—proper behavior and restraint.

It seems this Min Pin has made a new friend, just in time for the holidays.

Understanding the Dog's Language

Most authorities agree that the dog is a descendent of the wolf. The dog and wolf have similar traits. For instance both are pack oriented and prefer not to be isolated for long periods of time. Another characteristic is that the dog, like the wolf, looks to the leader—Alpha—for direction. Both the wolf and the dog communicate through body language, not only within their pack but with outsiders.

Every pack has an Alpha figure. The dog looks to you, or should look to you, to be that leader. If your dog doesn't receive the proper training and guidance, he very well may replace you as Alpha. This would be a serious problem and is certainly a disservice to your dog.

Eye contact is one way the Alpha wolf keeps order within his pack. You are Alpha so you must establish eye contact with your puppy. Obviously your puppy will have to look at you. Practice eye contact even if you need to hold his head for five to ten seconds at a time. You can give him a treat as a reward. Make sure

Making eye contact is essential in assuming the dominant role in the relationship with your dog and can be practiced for a few seconds at a time.

your eye contact is gentle and not threatening. Later, if he has been naughty, it is permissible to give him a long, penetrating look. I caution you there are some older dogs that never learned eye contact as puppies and cannot accept eye contact. You should avoid eye contact with these dogs since they feel threatened and will retaliate as such.

Body Language

The play bow, when the forequarters are down and the hindquarters are elevated, is an invitation to play. Puppies play fight, which helps them learn the acceptable limits of biting. This is necessary for later in their lives. Nevertheless, an owner may be falsely reassured by the playful nature of his dog's aggression. Playful aggression toward another dog or human may be an indication of serious aggression in the future.

151

Owners should never play fight or play tug-of-war with any dog that is inclined to be dominant.

Signs of submission are:
1. Avoids eye contact.
2. Active submission—the dog crouches down, ears back and the tail is lowered.
3. Passive submission—the dog rolls on his side with his hindlegs in the air and frequently urinates.

Signs of dominance are:
1. Makes eye contact.
2. Stands with ears up, tail up and the hair raised on his neck.
3. Shows dominance over another dog by standing at right angles over it.

Dominant dogs tend to behave in characteristic ways such as:
1. The dog may be unwilling to move from his place (i.e., reluctant to give up the sofa if the owner wants to sit there).
2. He may not part with toys or objects in his mouth and may show possessiveness with his food bowl.
3. He may not respond quickly to commands.
4. He may be disagreeable for grooming and dislikes to be petted.

Dogs are popular because of their sociable nature. Those that have contact with humans during the first 12 weeks of life regard them as a member of their own species—their pack. All dogs have the potential for both dominant and submissive behavior. Only through experience and training do they learn to whom it is appropriate to show which behavior. Not all dogs are concerned with dominance but owners need to be aware of that potential. It is wise for the owner to establish his dominance early on.

This Min Pin is showing total submission to her owner in the classic submissive position of laying on her back and completely exposing her belly.

Standing with the ears and tail up, as well as making eye contact, are signs of dominance. This fellow is just saying hello.

A human can express dominance or submission toward a dog in the following ways:

1. Meeting the dog's gaze signals dominance. Averting the gaze signals submission. If the dog growls or threatens, averting the gaze is the first avoiding action to take—it may prevent attack. It is important to establish eye contact in the puppy. The older dog that has not been exposed to eye contact may see it as a threat and will not be willing to submit.

2. Being taller than the dog signals dominance; being lower signals submission. This is why, when attempting to make friends with a strange dog or catch the runaway, one should kneel down to his level. Some owners see their dogs become dominant when allowed on the furniture or on the bed. Then he is at the owner's level

3. An owner can gain dominance by ignoring all the dog's

social initiatives. The owner pays attention to the dog only when he obeys a command.

No dog should be allowed to achieve dominant status over any adult or child. Ways of preventing are as follows:

1. Handle the puppy gently, especially during the three- to four-month period.
2. Let the children and adults handfeed him and teach him to take food without lunging or grabbing.
3. Do not allow him to chase children or joggers.
4. Do not allow him to jump on people or mount their legs. Even females may be inclined to mount. It is not only a male habit.
5. Do not allow him to growl for any reason.
6. Don't participate in wrestling or tug-of-war games.
7. Don't physically punish puppies for aggressive behavior. Restrain him from repeating the infraction and teach an alternative behavior. Dogs should earn everything they receive from their owners. This would include sitting to receive petting or treats, sitting before going out the door and sitting to receive the collar and leash. These types of exercises reinforce the owner's dominance.

Young children should never be left alone with a dog. It is important that children learn some basic obedience commands so they have some control over the dog. They will gain the respect of their dog.

FEAR

One of the most common problems dogs experience is being fearful. Some dogs are more afraid than others. On the lesser side, which is sometimes humorous to watch, my dog can be afraid of a strange object. He acts silly when something is out of place in the house. I call his problem perceptive intelligence. He realizes the abnormal within his known environment. He does not react the same way in strange environments since he does not know what is normal.

On the more serious side is a fear of people. This can result in backing off, seeking his own space and saying "leave me alone" or it can result in an aggressive behavior that may lead to challenging the person. Respect that the dog wants to be left alone and give him time to come forward. If you approach the cornered dog, he may resort to snapping. If you leave him alone, he may decide to come forward, which should be rewarded with a treat. Years ago we had a dog that behaved in this manner. We coaxed people to stop by the house and make friends with our fearful dog. She learned to take the treats and after weeks of work she overcame her suspicions and made friends more readily.

Some dogs may initially be too fearful to take treats. In these cases it is helpful to make sure the dog hasn't eaten for about 24 hours. Being a little hungry encourages him to accept the treats, especially if they are of the "gourmet" variety. I have a dog that worries about strangers since people seldom stop by my house. Over the years she has learned a cue and jumps up quickly to visit anyone sitting on the sofa. She learned by herself that all guests on the sofa were to be trusted friends. I think she felt more comfortable with them being at her level, rather than towering over her.

Dogs can be afraid of numerous things, including loud noises and thunderstorms. Invariably the owner rewards (by comforting) the dog when it shows signs of fearfulness. I had a terrible problem with my favorite dog in the Utility obedience class. Not only was he intimidated in the class but he was afraid of noise and afraid of displeasing me. Frequently he would knock down

Offering treats or reassurance to your Min Pin can be a way to alleviate fear of strange people or places.

the bar jump, which clattered dreadfully. I gave him credit because he continued to try to clear it, although he was terribly scared. I finally learned to "reward" him every time he knocked down the jump. I would jump up and down, clap my hands and tell him how great he was. My psychology worked, he relaxed and eventually cleared the jump with ease. When your dog is frightened, direct his attention to something else and act happy. Don't dwell on his fright.

AGGRESSION

Some different types of aggression are: predatory, defensive, dominance, possessive, protective, fear induced, noise provoked, "rage" syndrome (unprovoked aggression), maternal and aggression directed toward other dogs. Aggression is the most common behavioral problem encountered. Protective breeds are expected to be more aggressive than others but with the proper upbringing they can make very dependable companions. You need to be able to read your dog.

Many factors contribute to aggression including genetics and environment. An improper environment, which may include the living conditions, lack of social life, excessive punishment, being attacked or frightened by an aggressive dog, etc., can all influence a dog's behavior. Even spoiling him and giving too much praise may be detrimental. Isolation and the lack of human contact or exposure to frequent teasing by children or adults also can ruin a good dog.

Lack of direction, fear, or confusion lead to aggression in those dogs that are so inclined. Any obedience exercise, even the sit and down, can direct the dog and overcome fear and/or

Owners need to be able to know the differences between play-fighting, like this bitch and her puppies, and truly aggressive behavior.

Use the sit or down command if your dog is showing signs of dominance. Practicing these commands will let him know who's in charge.

confusion. Every dog should learn these commands as a youngster, and there should be periodic reinforcement.

When a dog is showing signs of aggression, you should speak calmly (no screaming or hysterics) and firmly give a command that he understands, such as the sit. As soon as your dog obeys, you have assumed your dominant position Aggression presents a problem because there may be danger to others. Sometimes it is an emotional issue. Owners may consciously or unconsciously encourage their dog's aggression. Other owners show responsibility by accepting the problem and taking measures to keep it under control. The owner is responsible for his dog's actions, and it is not wise to take a chance on someone being bitten, especially a child. Euthanasia is the solution for some owners and in severe cases this may be the best choice. However, few dogs are that dangerous and very few are that much of a threat to their owners. If caution is exercised and professional help is gained early on, then I surmise most cases can be controlled.

Some authorities recommend feeding a lower protein (less than 20 percent) diet. They believe this can aid in reducing aggression. If the dog loses weight, then vegetable oil can be added. Veterinarians and behaviorists are having some success with pharmacology. In many cases treatment is possible and can improve the situation.

If you have done everything according to "the book" regarding training and socializing and are still having a behavior problem, don't procrastinate. It is important that the problem gets attention before it is out of hand. It is estimated that 20 percent of a veterinarian's time may be devoted to dealing with problems before they become so intolerable that the dog is separated from its home and owner. If your veterinarian isn't able to help, he should refer you to a behaviorist.

My most important advice to you is to be aware of your dog's actions. Even so, remember dogs are dogs and will behave as such even though we might like them to be perfect little people. You and your dog will become neurotic if you worry about every little indiscretion. When there is reason for concern—don't waste time. Seek guidance. Dogs are meant to be loved and enjoyed.

References:

Manual of Canine Behavior, Valerie O'Farrell, British Small Animal Veterinary Association.

Good Owners, Great Dogs, Brian Kilcommons, Warner Books.

By being aware of your Min Pin's actions and reinforcing good behavior, you will both enjoy a happy and loving relationship.

RESOURCES

American Kennel Club
260 Madison Avenue
New York, New York 10016
or
5580 Centerview Drive
Raleigh, North Carolina 27606
919-233-3600
919-233-9767
www.akc.org

The Kennel Club
1 Clarges Street
Picadilly, London WIY 8AB, England

Canadian Kennel Club
100-89 Skyway Avenue
Etobicoke, Ontario, Canada M9W6R4

INDEX